Developing World-Class Organizations in a Rapidly Changing World

Rapid Retooling

Antoine Gerschel and Lawrence Polsky

16 15 14 13 1 2 3 4 5

ASTD Press is an internationally renowned source of insightful and practical information on workplace learning, performance, and professional development.

ASTD Press
1640 King Street Box 1443
Alexandria, VA 22313-1443 USA

Ordering information: Books published by ASTD Press can be purchased by visiting ASTD's website at store.astd.org or by calling 800.628.2783 or 703.683.8100.

Library of Congress Control Number: 2013931622
ISBN-10: 1-56286-864-0
ISBN-13: 978-1-56286-864-2
e-ISBN: 978-1-60728-544-1

ASTD Press Editorial Staff:
Director: Glenn Saltzman
Manager, ASTD Press: Ashley McDonald
Community of Practice Manager, Workforce Development: Ron Lippock
Associate Editor: Stephanie Castellano
Editorial Assistant: Sarah Cough
Text and Cover Design: Lon Levy

Printed by Victor Graphics, Inc., Baltimore, Maryland, www.victorgraphics.com.

Contents

Acknowledgments

We would first like to thank Sandy. Hurricane Sandy, that is. Sandy became the perfect example of a "rapid retooling" situation. In the final week of writing, three days before our manuscript was due, Sandy hit the East coast. We had planned to meet in New York City for three days to put the finishing touches on our book. Instead, without electricity and in the midst of chaos, we had to come up with a new writing process. Lawrence sat in his car so he could keep his phone—our substitute communication channel—charged, as we worked on restructuring and editing our chapters. While working on the book, we were also busy tending to the urgent needs of family and friends in the aftermath of the storm. In the end, we applied the tools in this book to keep focused and energized on our end goal. For that, we are thankful to Sandy for making rapid retooling even more relevant to us. Special thanks to Gerry and Marie Ruebenstahl, Alicia, Tim, and Ben Tate for their support during Sandy.

Secondly, this book would not exist without our adopted sister Anne Bruce. She connected us with Ron Lippock at ASTD. Bolstered by her encouragement, we pitched the idea and Ron loved it. Thank you, Anne, for your continued support of our literary and consulting endeavors. Stephanie Castellano got to know both our writing talents and—more importantly!—our limitations. Stephanie, for your advice, critical feedback, and patience through the editing process, thanks a million!

We also would like to thank the executives and organization leaders who let us share their stories about what it takes to succeed in a challenging business environment. There are too many to mention individually, but many of you will find yourselves in the book.

Writing a book is a huge undertaking that ultimately eats into the time and energy we dedicate to family. Our wives Noëmie and Teresa had to bear the brunt of family responsibilities, even during the aftermath of one of the worst hurricanes in the New York City area. This book, and in fact all our work success and world travels, could never have happened without you. We also want to thank our children, Misha, Ron, Giulia, Gretta, and Zach, who we hope through our example learn how to face life's challenges and seize all the terrific opportunities we have.

Antoine Gerschel

Lawrence Polsky

Preface

We have worked with and witnessed dozens of companies over the past five years that were forced to change quickly and on a large scale—whether due to economic, technological, or competitive challenges, or a change of leadership. These companies have had to find ways to *rapidly retool* themselves. Some have done so successfully, others not so well.

Encouraged by customers, business partners, and friends, we decided to collect our experiences and attempt to codify best practices for rapid retooling. The end result is this book. In these pages you will find real-world case studies, stories, and advice from executives who have led rapid change efforts. The book provides insights from world-class organizations, including Apple, Bayer, Beam Spirits, BMW Manufacturing, Cisco, Credit Suisse, EMC2, Enterasys Networks, Deloitte & Touche LLP, Faber-Castell USA, FedEx, Fisba, Google, ICON Clinical Research, Jiffy Lube/Shell, Make-A-Wish® International, McDonald's, Merck & Company, Merrimack Pharmaceuticals, NISC, Novartis, Infragistics, MacxRed, Nokia Mobile Payment Services, Puma, SAP, Skyline Exhibits, Staples, Starbucks, Orange Regional Medical Center, United States Patent and Trademark Office, St. Luke's Health System, Tenneco, the NYC Department of Health, UBS, Xcelris Labs, and more.

The stories are enjoyable and educational. However, ultimately you will need to figure out how to apply the ideas in the book to your own company. To help you, we have included:

- **Rapid Retooling Worksheets.** These are tools to help you implement the ideas outlined in the book in your organization.
- **Rapid Retooling Research.** We highlight research studies we believe are particularly relevant to our readers.
- **Rapid Retooling Recommendations.** These are specific recommendations from us or the executives we interviewed, to help you rapidly retool your organization.

We now present you with the lessons learned by real-life organizations and their leaders. We hope you both enjoy and benefit from the advice in this book.

Chapter 1
The Case for Rapid Retooling

John was born in a remote village in Turkey to parents of no education and no means. His childhood was spent in the midst of civil war that led to the splintering of his family and launched him into a life of destitution. He eventually found safety and solace in a seminary in Jerusalem, but after getting caught up in a different type of war abroad, he was banished back to Turkey where he became a fugitive of the Turkish Secret Service. But John had other aspirations for his life besides being a political outcast. Since childhood, he dreamed of being a doctor. He also wanted to one day live in the United States.

John made both dreams a reality. He moved to America and went to Columbia University for his undergraduate degree and Tufts University School of Medicine in Boston for his medical degree. A board-certified internist, he eventually entered the business world and worked his way up to the C-level team of a leading global pharmaceutical company. He now reshapes their high-level operations just as he reshaped his life: with vision and accountability. He is the epitome of a rapid retooler.

We know this introduction reads more like the summary of a novel than a business book. (In fact, John's life *is* the subject of his novel *Gray Wolves and White Doves.*) We have threaded John's story throughout this chapter because he is representative of many of the rapid retoolers we have worked with over the years; organizational leaders who faced seemingly unconquerable challenges and pushed on, despite the pressure and the resistance, in order to help their organizations survive a rapidly changing business landscape.

What Is Rapid Retooling?

Simply put, rapid retooling is what successful organizations are doing to keep ahead of the rapid pace of change. They respond to technological and economic pressures by quickly refocusing, retraining, and reenergizing their employees to achieve results.

You don't change an engine when you just need a different screwdriver. You don't need a new manufacturing line each time you are introducing a new production batch or a modified product. All you do is retool your manufacturing equipment. The same is true with people. People who adapt to external circumstances, constantly develop their skills, and regularly update their knowledge are retooling themselves.

Their employers retain them in order to leverage their knowledge, talent, skills, experience, and network, which enrich over time and compound their ability to give back to their organizations. Retaining these kinds of employees is certainly much more efficient than rehiring. Companies become dynamic organisms, retooling themselves in lockstep with the changing market.

RR Research: What CEOs Are Saying

An April 2012 study by Forbes and BMO Harris of 300 senior executives, called "Forbes Insights: Inspired for Growth," stresses a key finding about "middle market companies." Two-thirds of the executives surveyed say that in today's economy, companies have to continuously change and adapt their strategic course. One-third even talks about the need to revamp business models to enable growth.

The 2012 IBM Global CEO Study came to similar conclusions. They found that 67 percent of CEOs worldwide think their current business models are only sustainable for three years, and 21 percent think they are not sustainable after five years. This means that 88 percent of CEOs believe their business models will last five years at most!

Here are some samples of what we've heard from industry experts:

"The traditional pharmaceutical models are not working anymore. In recent years it reached a point where 'big pharma' had to come to grips with it. The pipeline challenges are immense, therapeutic approaches are moving away from small-molecule compounds to protein-based treatments which many companies are not set up for, and there is a huge focus on high cost of healthcare. Third-party payers are more dominant in the market, which brings along cost controls and a growing focus on patient outcomes. The management of costs has also brought about an acceptance and expectation for the use of generic drugs. It is a survival struggle for the traditional pharmaceutical companies!"

Mark Quigley, PhD

Senior VP, Global Quality and Compliance, ICON Clinical Research

"Most top-line growth is coming from emerging markets. There are two big issues with that: First, this growth comes at a high cost in terms of lower profit margin expectations. Second, the talent gap is huge—attracting and retaining the talent we need is a significant challenge in these markets."

Executive at a leading healthcare products company

"Each year gets faster and faster, but the pace is blistering this year [2012]. In fact, we are still calling audibles as the holiday season unfolds."

Corporate manager at a leading retail chain

We once had the pleasure of hearing Bob Johansen speak, the noted futurist author of *Leaders Make the Future: Ten New Leadership Skills for an Uncertain World*. He borrows the term *VUCA* from the U.S. Army to describe the current world we live in. Aptly applied to the current business landscape, the acronym stands for:

- *Volatile:* There is a high rate of change.
- *Uncertain:* Many things are unclear.
- *Complex:* There are more factors to consider.
- *Ambiguous:* There are mixed meanings.

RR Recommendation

Is your organization experiencing the elements of VUCA? We suggest these general approaches.

- *High Volatility:* Prioritize business goals so employees know where to focus their energies.
- *High Uncertainty:* Applaud mistakes so employees know that you want them to take risks despite operating in an uncertain environment.
- *High Ambiguity:* Continually clarify goals, strategies, responsibilities, processes, and factors influencing decisions.
- *High Complexity:* Break down decisions, projects, and problem-solving processes into smaller chunks to help employees tackle them.

Whether you are in a declining market or a growing one, your company is challenged to quickly adapt. Companies in declining markets are being forced to reevaluate their products and services. They are asking their leaders to cut costs, innovate, and reposition. They need to refocus their resources on areas that are profitable. Companies in growing markets are faced with finding and retaining talent, and managing profitability while maintaining quality. At either end, or anywhere in between, organizations need to adapt quickly, either to stave off decline or manage growth. We call this process *rapid retooling.*

The Fast Pace of Change

The pace of technology changes can be gleaned from these statistics from the U.S. Patent & Trademark Office. The number of patent applications nearly doubled in about 30 years from 1963 to 1990. In

the next 10 years it nearly doubled again. In the 10 years after that, it increased 60 percent. To keep with up with the pace of change, the Patent Office is in the midst of retooling its system of reviewing and granting patents. The U.S. Congress passed the America Invents Act in 2011, forcing an overhaul of the system.

Figure 1-1. Number of Patent Applications

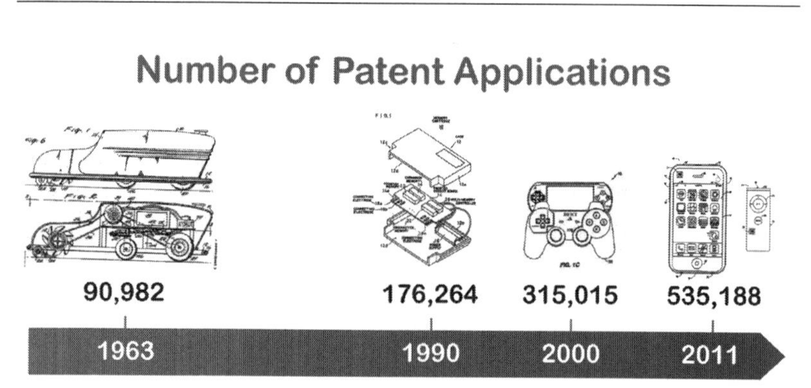

Five Requirements for Rapid Retooling

When you say "organizational change," people often think of layoffs, mergers, acquisitions, or new enterprise-wide computer systems. And for many organizations, that is what change means: cost cuts, improved processes, and new technology. But change can also mean new leadership, the launch of a new product, a new strategic direction, expansion into other markets, or organization-wide problems of any nature.

Usually a lot of time and money goes into new technology, processes, and tools during times of change. But the "soft" requirements for change to succeed are often only considered after major problems develop. Unfortunately, these soft requirements are perceived as less important than numbers and hard facts. We forget that they have a

RR Research: Concurrent Change Initiatives

In 2011 PeopleNRG began conducting a yearly global survey to investigate trends in change leadership around the globe. It consists of 18 questions, answered by 550 professionals from nearly 50 countries. One of the questions asked is, "How many change projects are you involved in?" Both years, 62 percent of respondents said they are involved in three or more concurrent change initiatives at work.

Figure 1-2. Concurrent Change Initiatives

0 PROJECTS

5+ PROJECTS 21%

1-2 PROJECTS 35%

3-4 PROJECTS 41%

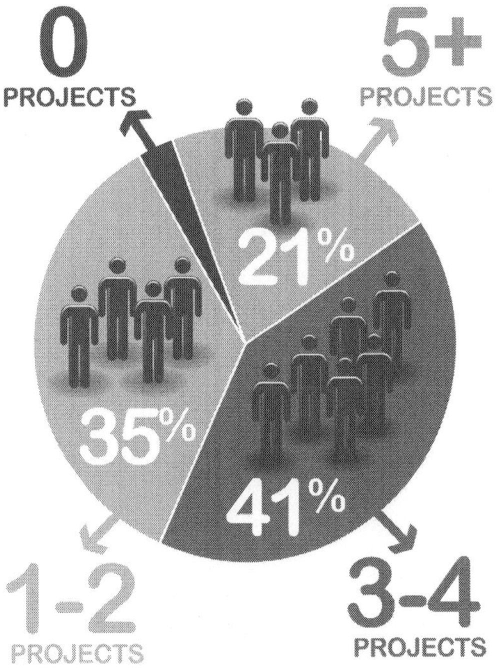

direct impact on the ultimate success of our change initiatives. In our work we have identified five soft requirements for rapid change efforts to be successful:

1. building business acumen
2. creating a culture of innovation
3. busting down silos
4. energizing your team
5. making it personal.

Everyone knows that change at work is considered negative. It is disruptive and very emotional. Invariably it results in reduced morale and productivity, at least initially, because it is emotionally straining on employees and leaders alike. Yet our work with customers has led us to an important observation: It takes the same amount of effort, risk, and emotional strain to manage success as it does to manage negative changes that involve restructuring, downsizing, and the like.

Therefore this book focuses on dealing with change that stems from success and growth, as well as "negative" change. It offers strategies for employees and leaders to stay focused and reenergize themselves and their teams around continually changing business strategies, so that they ultimately position themselves and their organizations for success.

Book Overview

John's story (which we began at the start of this chapter) illustrates the key points in this book. John met each of the five requirements for successful rapid retooling—during his turbulent youth and later in life as a corporate executive—and the story of how he did so will help you understand them.

Chapter 2: Building Business Acumen. The first requirement for rapid retooling is to get employees to understand and focus on the business. The case examples in this chapter show firsthand how leaders are accomplishing this. We provide several suggestions for learning the business of your business.

John was hired as a senior vice president at an international, U.S.-based pharmaceutical corporation. He was two levels below the CEO in an organization of more than 100,000 employees. His main focus was patient safety and regulatory affairs. From the first time anything was tested on a human, through the investigational phase, the approval, and as long the product was on the market, his area had to make sure that proper regulations and laws were followed; if there were any safety issues, the company responded quickly.

John was hired because the organization was under serious scrutiny from governing agencies who considered customer safety in jeopardy. Upon beginning his position, John remarked, "The current workflow was more complicated than the New York City subway map. On top of that, for each area—oncology, consumer health, vaccines—there was a different process taking a different amount of time." When he arrived, the company was in month eight of a 12-month feasibility study, having already spent $5,000,000 to determine the feasibility of changing the process for responding to safety issues. After the study was complete, it was projected to take three years to fully implement the change. John's job was to find a way to do this faster and more cost-effectively.

So he brought his team together and asked two simple questions: "Do you agree that you have to change the process?" They all said yes. Then he asked, "Are there any arguments or qualifiers regarding that?" They all said no. So he asked the obvious: "Then why are you doing a feasibility study for a whole year at the cost of over $8,000,000, and then anticipate three years and tens of millions more dollars to actually make the change?" Their answer: "That's how things are done here."

John explained that they couldn't wait three years to sort this out. He gave them two weeks to come back with a six-month plan to change the process.

Here is a very interesting side story about this dilemma: In John's first encounter with the CEO at an executive team meeting, the first thing the CEO said was, "Don't bother." "Excuse me?" John asked. The CEO responded, "Every time a new person gets in your spot, they come to me and say, I need $200 million to fix this. And guess what, these are safety and compliance issues. There's nothing we can do but give him or her the $200 million. I know you're going to do the same thing."

John said, "No, this is different. I don't want any money. I just need you to listen and support what I do. There are no additional resources that I'm going to request. I don't promise, but when this is done, I believe we will need fewer resources." He immediately had the CEO on his side.

John clearly had business acumen and used it to focus on the business issues. He knew it was unwise for the business to spend hundreds of millions of dollars and years to solve the problem. When people started objecting that it couldn't be done in six months he told them, "Think of the cost to maintain all these processes for three years while we come up with a new one, versus for six months. The cost avoidance is immeasurable."

He sharpened his team's focus on the end-goal by giving them a short timeline (we will expand on the importance of this in chapter 2) and by giving them three priorities while devising their plan. First, it had to be a very simple, linear process. Second, he insisted that the new process be the same for all product areas, functions, and geographic regions. Third, the process should stipulate completion of deliverables in a three-day timeframe. Before, resolving safety issues would have been given a deadline of up to 30 days, if not placed in backlog, where they could remain unsolved for up to a year!

Chapter 3: Fostering Innovation. Innovation is not always about blowing up the box. Sometimes it is about defining the box's parameters in a different way. In addition to the business cases in this chapter, we provide practical innovation tools you can use to foster a creative environment. This chapter also focuses on the importance of understanding customers' needs and problems; creating an environment of trust to allow for mistakes; and how to handle conflict effectively.

John, by giving his team a clear framework within which they had to work, was able to channel their innovation into more efficient results. "When the team came back in two weeks, they had a presentation with six slides that described the six-month plan for change. And then they had about 60 slides outlining the risks! Sixty!" He patiently listened to them and discussed their key points. At the end he said, "There are only three risks that would make me consider stopping this project or entertaining delays. Number one, patients' health: If what we're doing would put any patient at risk, that's an immediate stop. Number two, regulatory risk: If you show me at any time that the compliance issue is worsening, we have to change. Number three is legal risk: If for legal reasons we cannot do something, then we stop. Nothing else matters. I will take personal accountability for these decisions; you will take accountability for hitting the six-month deadline."

Redefining their parameters in this way, and removing some of the obstacles they perceived, freed John's team members to think of new, viable solutions for improving the process.

Chapter 4: Overcoming Silo Thinking. To rapidly retool, organizations need to break down boundaries surrounding each function. In this chapter we explore several keys to busting silos, including how to use common goals to unite cross-functional employees, physically integrating functions to facilitate their collaboration, and how to collaborate on decision-making processes.

When we asked John to reflect on breaking down silos, he says that was his biggest challenge. He explained, "At this high level in the organization, your peers aim for the lowest common denominator and expect you to play by those rules. They don't want standouts. There is a lot of competition in the areas of socializing with the C-level suite, but not in delivery. If one person succeeds, the rest look bad. There is a lot of undermining each other's projects at this level. They tried to undermine my initiative, claiming that I was going to put the company at risk. And the next thing I know, lawyers are all over me. That happened throughout the project."

How did he bust the silos? He stuck to the business mission. Challenged his challengers. Kept and cultivated the support of his boss. Eventually, most (not all) of his peers begrudgingly accepted his accomplishments.

Chapter 5: Energizing Teams. A common question we get is, "How do you keep employee morale up during periods of rapid change?" The truth is you can't keep morale up. No matter what you do, employee morale will take a hit. Employees will find it difficult to stay upbeat and productive. This chapter presents strategies and tools that organizational leaders use to keep morale up as much as possible while rapidly retooling. We look at how the skills and confidence of the leader has a huge impact, how it is important to match the team structure to work needs, and finally how the simple act of celebrating accomplishments makes a huge difference.

There were a few things that helped John's team stay energized. As we mentioned earlier, the short timeframe helped. "I have found that any project longer than six months becomes a drag on team energy," John remarked. "That was one of the reasons I made the deadline six months." People like to experience progress and know that the end is in sight. They feel energized when they see results. "My team started seeing that we were gradually making progress; that the system was falling into place. As they saw the results, they started taking pride in them and working harder. They started becoming believers."

Did John's rapid retooling succeed? "We have a lot of metrics we track. Before this project, our performance ranged from 30 percent to 80 percent, depending on the measure. For compliance, it was very, very poor. But within the first few months after the go-live, all these measures jumped to about 95 percent. After a few more months, they went above 99 percent. Before this project, we had tens of thousands of backlogged issues that sometimes took over 100 days to resolve. Now, 99 percent of the cases are solved in three days."

Chapter 6: Making It Personal. The age of work-life balance is passed. To thrive in today's rapidly changing world, organizations need to integrate employee interests with the organizational mission. Leaders especially need to have passion for the mission of the organization. This kind of engagement is necessary for successful rapid retooling. Additionally, this chapter explores how much control to give employees in their work, and personal attributes of rapid retoolers.

In John's case, he had forged a successful career out of change. In job after job he recreated processes and procedures to enable his employers to succeed. His passion lay in re-charting paths to the companies' success. The change initiative he led at the multinational pharma company was successful; however, 5 percent of employees chose to leave as a result.

John said, "I can't see any lack of intelligence or capability in those who had to drop out. I think they just were too entrenched in their ways, too resistant to change, and couldn't retool their thinking or their willingness to change." To operate at this level successfully requires rapid—and constant—retooling. You cannot be in a job that requires you to lead change if you are not naturally inclined to it, in your personal life as well as your professional life.

RR Recommendation

John says forget the consultants. It's not the models you use or the consultants you pay—it comes down to the leader. To accomplish rapid retooling, you need a leader who believes in it, wants to do it, is determined to do it, has a clear vision and a clear path, and then one way or another, is able to bring everyone onboard.

Chapter 7: Rapid Retooling in a High-Tech, Multicultural World. We have included a final chapter outlining examples of how to use the training function to rapidly retool your organization. In today's world of global business and virtual teams, organizations have to learn how to rapidly retool in creative ways. It is not as simple as an edict, or offering a class in one location. Cases from Google, Cisco, Shell Oil, and others show you how leading companies are doing it.

RR Research: Don't Wait for HR

In September 2012, Lumesse, a talent management solutions company, surveyed 769 human resources executives around the globe, and found that 82 percent of respondents (74 percent from the U.S.) believe that employees have to learn more and faster to succeed than they did five years ago. Fifty-one percent of HR leaders worldwide and 38 percent in the U.S. said they are some way from delivering to their full potential when it comes to providing employees with the right training and knowledge for their roles. Furthermore, results indicated that the majority of employees see their colleagues as a more valuable resource for learning new skills than their internal learning management systems.

Worksheet: Are You Ready to Rapidly Retool?

Use this worksheet to determine which soft requirement for change your organization needs to focus on most.

	Low		High
Building Business Acumen:	No Business Sense	↔	MBA Mindset
Creating an Innovative Culture:	Risk-Averse	↔	Fearless
Busting Down Silos:	Silos Dominate	↔	Collaborative
Energizing Your Team:	Slow to Action	↔	Empowered
Making It Personal:	Disengaged; Burnt-out	↔	Engaged; Passionate

Chapter 2
Building Business Acumen

Learning the Business of Your Business

"We are not in the training and development business. We are in the business of business." This remark by Bob Bennett, CLO of FedEx Express, is true for any function in any company, especially training and development. It must be focused on the business issues for the organization as a whole to succeed in today's challenging environment. This chapter looks at several practical examples of how organizations are finding ways to do this.

One of Bennett's first steps as CLO and HR VP at FedEx Express was to articulate and communicate his values, which he did with the acronym PIECES! These values became the driving force to retool all of their training and HR services.

Bennett knew he had to rapidly change things. Not that their training wasn't good. In fact it was world-class. They had received numerous awards for top-quality training. But as Bennett said, "I didn't want to have the world's best training or hiring process. What I really wanted was to integrate learning and development into daily practices at FedEx so that we met our overarching business goals."

The principles upon which FedEx operates are people, service, and profit. Everything Bennett's department did had to benefit those three areas. They could no longer afford to have great training for great training's sake. It had to drive better service and more profit. The training department's PIECES! values are therefore clearly linked to FedEx's company values:

- **P** – Partner with our customers. This means making their goals our goals. We can't partner if we don't hold ourselves accountable to their bottom-line success.
- **I** – Increase flexibility. Customers don't want to hear "no." If a customer has a problem, we need to be the one-stop solution. If we cannot find an answer, we need to find out who can. Innovation is not always about an "a-ha" moment, but about being open and flexible to small improvements.
- **E** – Expand our sphere of influence. This means getting involved in and leading organizations outside the company: industry organizations, governmental organizations, community organizations. It is imperative that we are driving change and organizational agendas rather than reacting to them, and that we are building the relationships necessary for us to successfully operate and prosper in a complex and interdependent environment.

- **C** – Calculate value-add. We have lots of demands. We have to prioritize what to take on. We won't entertain anything for which we cannot determine a value-add in terms of people, service, or profit, because we need to stay focused on the business goals.
- **E** – Enhance the training department's reputation. Increase visibility; get out there. You can't design a course unless you have been on the truck, sorting packages, loading packages on airplanes. This kind of involvement also enhances our trust and credibility within the organization.
- **S** – Sustain results. Stay focused on business outcomes. If you do your job right and provide value, no one wants to live without your services.
- **!** – Reminder that nothing gets done without our people. People make things happen. Provide the right environment and development opportunities for them so they can excel.

The View From the Ground

Lawrence was speaking to a manager of talent management at one of the nation's leading utility companies last summer. A strike was going on. And as so often during strikes, the managers had to fill the workers' roles. This manager was doing commercial meter reading for four weeks. He said, "I now can do a great job consulting to this division because of that experience. I really understand their business from the ground level!"

What are some creative ways you can learn the business of your business? See chapter 7 for more suggestions from Google, Beam, BMW, FedEx, and Puma.

RR Recommendation

"I was the fourth engineer hired into the company. The first thing that I did in my new position was move my office from the corporate headquarters to the Memphis station, where they do the pickup and deliveries, because I didn't know anything about this company and needed to learn from the source. I spent almost a year doing my job from the Memphis station. I helped them sort packages, and load and unload. And to this day, when I go talk to anyone in that part of the organization, they think I was in operations. If I make a suggestion to the operators, they listen because they believe I was an operator. It gave me instant credibility. So, that's one thing I really stress: Learn the business—however you can."

Bob Bennett, CLO, FedEx

Prioritizing Your Priorities

Beam, one of the world's leading premium spirits companies, is extremely business-focused. They recognize the value of getting people focused on the bottom line. When a new CEO, Matthew Shattock, started in 2009, he wanted all 3,300 employees working towards the same goals. So he did something simple. He created a one-page "Vision Into Action" sheet. This sheet includes:

- vision statement
- mission statement
- financial objectives for the year
- cultural values
- top 10 priorities
- three key performance indicators.

According to Sue Gannon, Vice President of Talent, Culture, and Organization Development at Beam, the beauty of this sheet is that it did what it set out to do. "Everyone started hanging it on their office walls. This way, it is always there to keep you focused on the business priorities."

Worksheet: What's Important to Your Business?

- What is your company's vision?

  ____

  ____

- What is your team's mission?

  ____

  ____

- What are the financial objectives for the year?

  ____

  ____

- What are your cultural values?

  ____

  ____

- What are your team's top priorities?

  ____

  ____

- What are the top three key performance indicators of success?

  ____

  ____

Jason Jennings, in his book *The Reinventors*, talks about how focusing on a few things differentiates high-performing companies from average performers. He mentions research conducted by the Hackett Group, a global strategic consulting company, which found that lower-performing organizations focus on an average of 372 priorities a year. Higher-performing companies, on average, focus on 21.

The message is, "Don't get bogged down with too many projects." Recently a senior leader of one our client organizations remarked, "That is all fine. But we are changing our whole organization. How can we focus on only three, five, or even 10 priorities?" It was simple, really. We helped him identify the top five priorities that would make his division successful within the context of the larger changes going on.

At executive team meetings we often ask everyone to write down their top five priorities. We then go around the room and have each team member read his answers. Guess what? They all have different priorities. Then we ask the leaders of the teams to read their lists. While they do have a few that their executive teams have listed, they also have others the teams don't even know about. This is too common. As a leader, don't assume anything is obvious to your employees. You have to relentlessly make your priorities clear, so that your team understands them and can articulate them.

Understanding P&L

Beyond understanding priorities and objectives, having business acumen also means understanding how money is made. Sue Gannon describes why this is important at Beam: "One of our values is entrepreneurialism—'thinking and acting like an owner'—so we need to help people build the skills and competencies to do that. Our top value-creating leaders got together last year and decided that we needed to

Worksheet: Synch Up Your Priorities

Our team's top five priorities are:

1. ____

2. ____

3. ____

4. ____

5 ____.

Ask your team members to write down what they each consider as the team's top five priorities. Then share the responses (without unduly embarrassing anyone) at the next team meeting. Especially note the manager's list of priorities compared to others.

create commercial focus at all levels. We want people to have commercial breadth—not just depth. Given the competitive nature of our market, we need our people to respond quickly with new ideas and approaches. They need to be able to independently make decisions, innovate, and take risks. To do this successfully, they need to understand the commercial consequence of what we do. They need to understand profit and loss: how we make and spend money. Traditionally P&L was owned by finance. Not anymore. All financial information is being shared. Our people at all levels need to understand the finance side, so we can continue to make the right decisions quickly, decisions based on a solid understanding of the business. The goal is that if there is a scenario in which we are discussing a decision, everyone involved can talk about how it links back to the P&L."

To learn more about how Beam taught their people about the P&L, see chapter 7.

RR Recommendation

Mike Michalowicz, serial entrepreneur and author of *Toilet Paper Entrepreneur* and *The Pumpkin Plan*, suggests a five-minute huddle with your team. Once a week, a person is assigned to share his latest business knowledge. It could be something he learned on the job, while collaborating with a colleague or supplier, or from an article or book.

Making Change Personal

Leaders need to go further than acquiring business acumen. They need to make business personal, especially during times of rapid change. As Martin Huber, CFO of Fisba Optik, a world leader in optical systems and components, puts it: "Change comes with bad feelings because people expect bad news. There is doubt and suspicion. You can't force people to change. You need to give them a good enough reason to change so that they do it on their own. You need to explain why this is happening, what the business reason is, and what happens if we don't do it. Make it personal—what would it mean for them if they can't or won't adjust?"

For example, if we asked you to get up tomorrow at 2 a.m., wake your family, go outside immediately and cross the street, would you?

We have asked this question of leaders around the world and 99 percent say no. Why? It is really inconvenient and they get nothing out of it. That is how employees feel about the changes you are implementing. And that is the reason nothing happens. When we ask the same leaders, "Would you do it if your house was on fire?" of course they all say yes!

You need to create a personal, emotional reason for people to change. This starts with sharpening employees' business acumen. With that acumen, they know why they should get out of bed at 2 a.m.

Once we were in a meeting with Jesse Singer, Deputy Commissioner of PCIP (Primary Care Information Project), a bureau within the NYC Department of Health, and his team, which was experiencing morale problems. Team members were frustrated because they felt their work had become about getting compliance with their new system. He explained to them, "I know sometimes it feels like we are just tracking numbers. But those numbers help save lives. For example, for the first time we can track blood pressure by race across NYC. This lets us see any differences, which we can then explore, understand, and help. This is public health. This is our business, our reason for being here. And we couldn't do it without all this work to get compliance with our systems." The message got through to a manager on his team, Vitaliy Shtutin, who said after a meeting, "This will really help motivate the team. They'll be reminded of how our work helps improve public health."

Leaders often have a hard time making the case for change. To get people truly on board with change takes a sales pitch. If you can't articulate the reasons for it clearly and convincingly, you will have a difficulty implementing the change.

Once we led a workshop at a global manufacturing company that was reorganizing itself. After a senior executive gave a 30-minute presentation on the changes, we asked the other attendees to summarize what they heard was changing. They had a hard time feeding back the main reasons, even though this wasn't the first time they had heard the presentation.

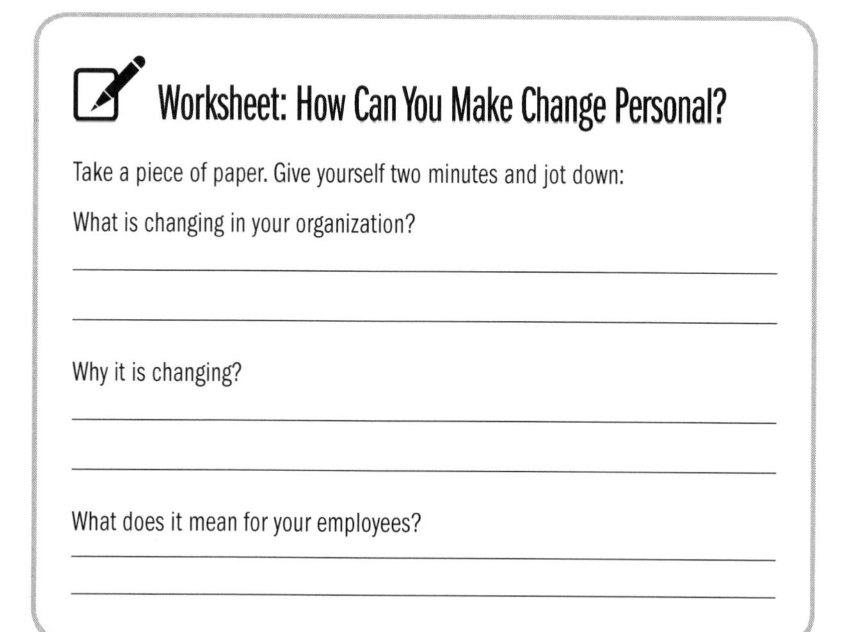
Worksheet: How Can You Make Change Personal?

Take a piece of paper. Give yourself two minutes and jot down:

What is changing in your organization?

____

____

Why it is changing?

____

____

What does it mean for your employees?

____

____

From that point on, we have had leaders work on constructing their own change speeches. We introduced a PeopleNRG tool called "The One-Minute Change Speech" that would help leaders sell the change. There are three parts:

- *What is changing?* These are the specifics of what will change. The purpose of this section of the speech is to give people concrete examples of the implications the change holds for them.
- *Why is it changing?* This is where you make the business case for change. A good "why" statement will increase employees' sense of urgency to change. It will also help people stay motivated through the challenges they face as the change is implemented. Maybe the "why" is to save money, maybe it is to beat the competition, or maybe it is to help people work more efficiently together. Whatever it is, you need to tell your employees about it.

- *What is not changing?* Sharing all the things that aren't changing—the values, reporting relationships, certain responsibilities—gives employees a sense of stability in the midst of chaos. Franz Aatz, founder of the start-up MacxRed, a developer of trading technologies, sees the importance of focusing on what is *not* changing. "When we introduce change, it pushes people out of their comfort zone. They feel exposed and unsafe. So if you can create an area of safety in the change, it will ease their distress. This is why you want to tell people what is not changing, to remind them that an element of stability exists."

Another example of making change personal occurred at the Orange County Medical Center, in Middletown, New York. They had a plan to change the face of healthcare in the region, which included merging two hospitals at a brand-new facility. They moved about 2,400 staff, a team of about 500 doctors, and a volunteer staff of around 400. Before the physical move, they implemented a new electronic health record system. This affected all the doctors and over half of the staff.

They spent a lot of time and energy explaining why this change was important for the healthcare providers and patients. "Why does this matter? And what's in it for me? These were critical questions to answer," said Jonnie Wesley-Krueger, Director of Training and Education. "Particularly because medical professionals are very task-focused. 'You had better tell me why I have to do this; otherwise I'm not going to be very happy.' We spent a great deal of time talking about the electronic health record and what it meant for patient safety, patient care, and access to patient information. 'What are the benefits? It's going to make everybody uncomfortable so why are we doing this?'

"First and foremost, we talked about the increase in patient safety the new health records would bring about. One of the benefits of an electronic health record is automatic prompts or flags that draw users' attention to potential patient allergies or other concerns, therefore reducing the incidents of medical errors.

"The second benefit we talked about was more accessible information. For example, let's say we have to do a blood draw. In the old days, we would have had to physically transport the blood specimen to the lab, have them analyze it, write up their report, and then physically send the information back upstairs. Now, we take the specimen at the bedside and use a pneumatic tube system to ship it downstairs. The lab then processes it, enters the results in the electronic health record, and in about a third or a quarter of the time we have the information as to what's going on. It expedites everything. Staff members don't have to physically pull the films or the reports."

The first change to the new health record prepared employees for the bigger change to the new building. "We had people who had spent their entire careers in one building. And we were teasing them about it during the orientation programs—'You survived the change to the health record, now we are just moving you into a place where you're not going to know where the bathroom is.' We implemented two major changes, in terms of people's day-to-day functioning, during a span of less than six months. It was a lot. But they handled it very well."

Now that we explained what it means to make business personal, go back to the worksheet *How Can You Make Change Personal?* What can you add or adjust? Once you think it is complete, practice with a peer or ask your manager if they have any input. Practice will make you better prepared for when you need to address employee concerns or frustration during the change.

The Value of Values

As we mentioned, a key strategy for helping employees manage their fears during change is to remind them about what is *not* changing. Company values are probably the most stable, unchanging elements of a company. Knowing and owning company values allows employees to have direction and know their boundaries. Should they focus on speed? Accuracy? Collaboration? Knowing and living company values increases productivity during ambiguous times.

Google has their "10 Things We Know to Be True." Zappos has their "10 Family Core Values." And Apple had Steve Jobs. He recognized that values drive culture. So before he died, he created Apple University, where employees can learn about the company's corporate values through case studies and key "historic" events at Apple.

When Tim Cook took over as CEO of Apple, he responded directly to concerns that Apple could not survive without Steve Jobs by calling upon the company values: "The values of our company are extremely well entrenched. We believe that we're on the face of the earth to make great products and that's not changing. We're constantly focusing on innovating. We believe in the simple, not the complex. We believe that we need to own and control the primary technologies behind the products that we make. And participate only in markets where we can make a significant contribution. We believe in saying "no" to thousands of projects so that we can really focus on the few that are truly important and meaningful to us. We believe in deep collaboration and cross-pollenization of our groups, which allow us to innovate in ways that others cannot. And frankly, we don't settle for anything less than excellence in every group in the company—and we have the self-honesty to admit when we're wrong and the courage to change. And I think regardless of who is in what job, those values are so embedded in this company that Apple will do extremely well."

Changing Values to Deal With Change

Despite the fact that values provide an element of stability, there are situations when companies decide to change their values based on new business challenges. Staples was forced to reevaluate their values in recent years, and the change led all the way to increased profitability.

Staples is a start-up success story. Experiencing extremely rapid growth for 20 years, their retail stores spread around the globe. But they had outgrown their original values. With 90,000 employees in 27 countries, it was time to rapidly retool. Through strategic planning and an engagement survey in 2011, Staples realized that they needed to position themselves as a more innovative and flexible company.

"We ended up with a retail division that was very tightly managed and without a lot of creativity," said Kate Hyatt, Director of Talent Management and Organizational Development. "For example, with the move to online ordering, customers were buying from a variety of channels. But we had built a culture in which everyone was focused on their stores. We needed a broader mindset beyond just 'my store.' We needed to change the culture."

Hyatt continued, "We decided to focus on our company values as a way to change behavior. We have had the same values in place for 20 years during our growth phase. We were in a new phase and needed to change our focus."

The work culture was all about doing the "smart thing." Their management is full of smart, analytic people: Harvard MBAs and more than 100 black belts. But while this accounted for the company's early

Figure 2-1. Staples' Old Values

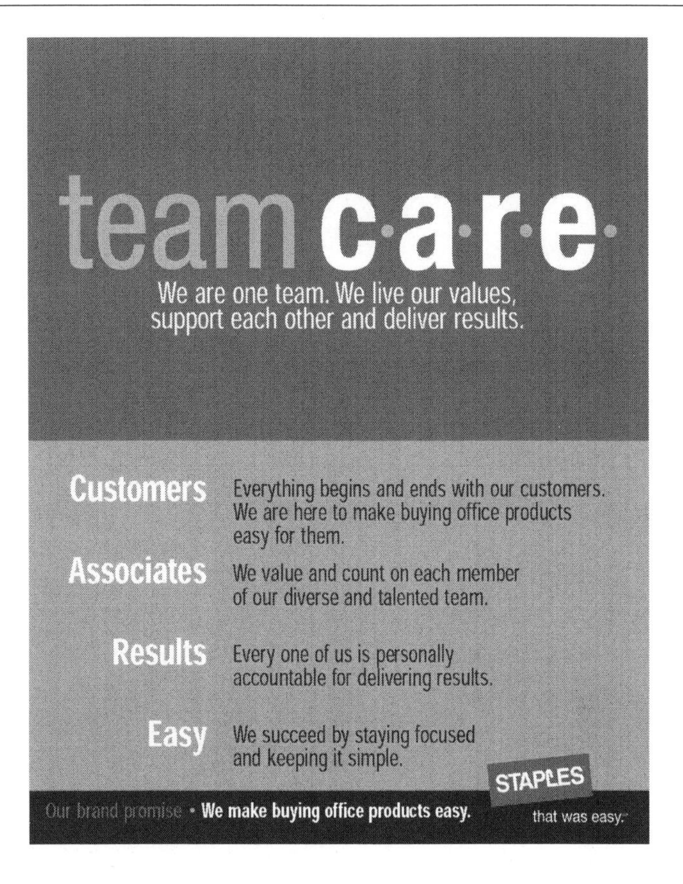

success, it was now an obstacle. As Hyatt said, "They tend to overanalyze things. We couldn't do much quickly. A turning point was when one of our senior leaders recommended a new approach. He suggested in one situation that we move ahead without much analysis or a pilot. He advocated 'progress over perfection.'"

They adopted this approach when considering a culture makeover. Instead of hiring consultants or having the leaders define the culture, they asked the employees. Instead of aiming for perfection, they aimed

Figure 2-2. Staples' New Values

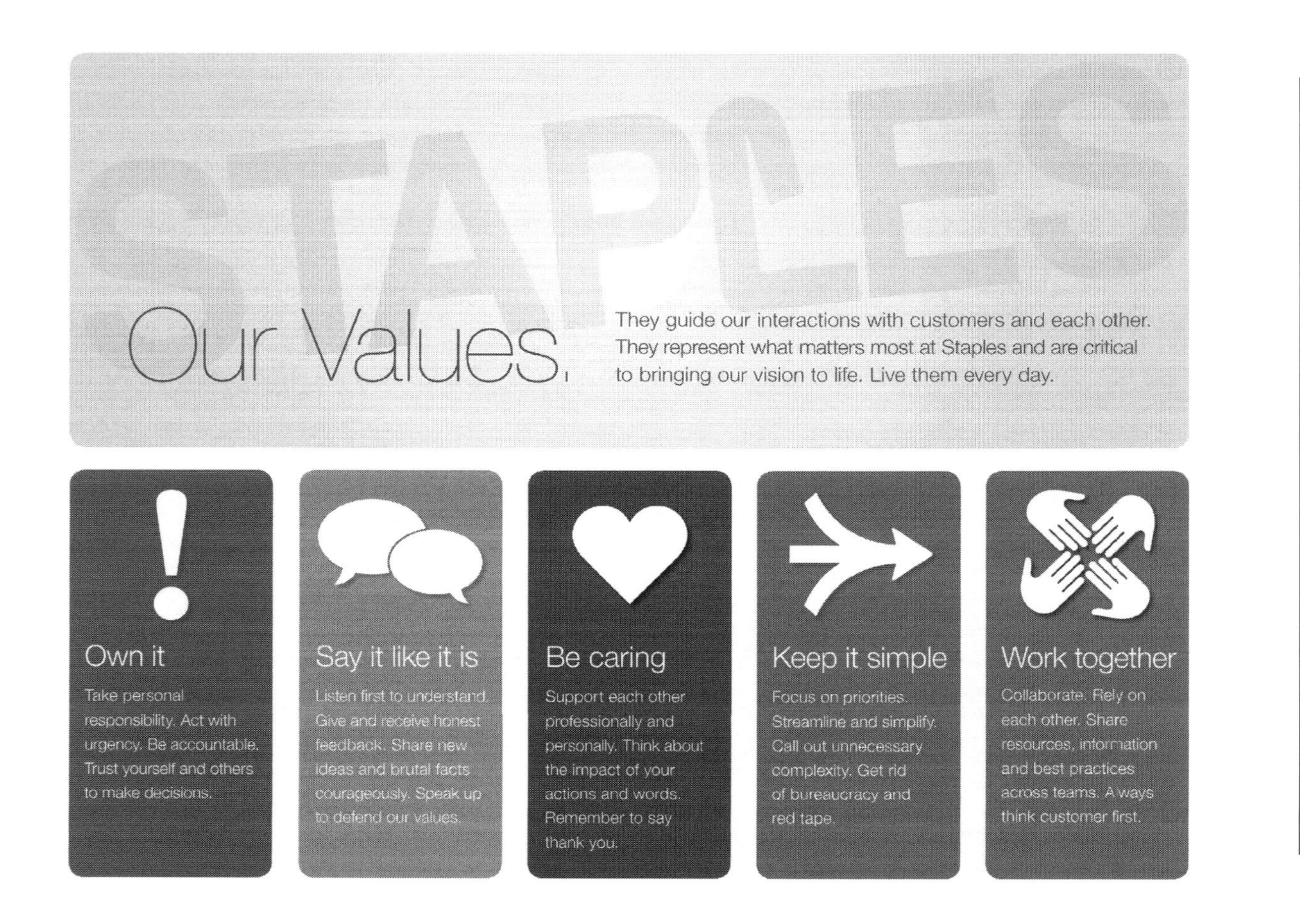

for a lot of input. They used social networks to conduct a values survey they called the "Values Jam." To market this initiative, they identified 70 employees as "Culture Connectors," employees who were perceived as strong informal leaders for their function or business unit. "The Culture Connectors helped get the word out. They developed their own posters and electronic documents to promote the Jam. Some used jelly jars, some used music, and some put 'graffiti posters' on public walls so employees could write down their thoughts in words and pictures about Staples' values.

"We didn't force people to do the survey," said Hyatt. "We wanted information only from people who wanted to participate. We ended with 15,000 respondents. We followed that up with 40 focus groups around the world to validate the data and explore geographic and business unit differences."

Talk about rapid retooling. The end result was the fastest organizational initiative of all time at Staples. The new values were identified, distributed online, and translated into 18 languages in 14 weeks.

The new values are behavioral. They are easy to apply. And they fit the new collaborative, innovative culture Staples needed to implement. The value "Say it like it is" is a great example. Hyatt told us, "People now use this value to preface their comments when they bring up issues and questions with higher-level people. They now say, 'I am uncomfortable with this approach,' or 'I have this idea.' That wouldn't have happened before."

Another example of changing values due to a major business challenge occurred at Swiss Re. An article in the *Schweizer Versicherung Online*, a Swiss online newsletter for insurance companies, describes how Swiss Re, the world's largest reinsurer, made a significant statement error in the second quarter of 2010. To address this error, the

RR Recommendation

Follow these five steps to clarify the values of your organization:

1. Identify a diverse group of 10 people in your organization. They can be from different functions, units, or geographies.
2. Explain the business challenges, triggering a values clarification process.
3. Ask them, "How do we need to behave in order to create a high-performing organization in the face of these challenges?"
4. Have each person find 10 more people and ask them the same question.
5. Collect all the responses and take a few hours with your team to identify trends and similarities.

company decided to not only revisit transaction flow, process tools, safety systems, and so forth, but to also look at soft factors. In this process they discovered that the Swiss Re finance department did not have a set of common values. As a result, the Swiss Re Group CFO, George Quinn, launched the "Finance as One" initiative with the explicit goal to introduce solid values and transform the department's culture. They went through a bottom-up and top-down values clarification process. Then they consecutively trained 70 ambassadors and 21 change leads around the globe who became in charge of promoting those new values locally and facilitating their practical implementation. Says Andreas Leu, the "Finance in One" Program Director, "We did not only renew and clarify the vision and strategy of the finance team, but at the same time created an attractive work environment for employees that motivated them to achieve higher performance levels."

Values in Government Organizations

Is there a place for values in government? Jesse Singer, the Deputy Commissioner of PCIP mentioned previously, thought so. "When I became leader of this bureau, I was reading about leading companies and I saw many of them had a strong focus on values. I thought, why not? Why not be a government entity that is considered a top-performing organization? We were also in the midst of significant changes. I was taking over and we were growing, so I thought values would give us common ground."

Singer got his 90 employees together and asked them, "What are the values we need to embody to be a great place to work?" They collected all the ideas and voted, choosing the top nine. They decided that these values would guide hiring and management practices, as well as daily behaviors.

- Be a "Collabosaurus."
- Create and Innovate—"Creatovate."
- Embody Humility and Equality.
- Awesome Is Contagious.
- People, Not Positions.
- No Right, No Wrong, Only Progress.
- Get Your Hands Dirty.
- Be Nerdy, Have Swagger.
- Be Passionate: Take Pride in What You Do.

Singer is finding the values very helpful in shaping the desired culture. "We have quarterly rewards for staff members who embody the values. Employees vote for each other, and those who best embody each of the values receive a small toy. For example, the winner of 'Get Your Hands Dirty' gets a Tonka dump trunk that sits on their desk for the quarter. The winner of 'Be a Collabosaurus' gets a stuffed dinosaur. The cool thing is that without offering money as a motivator, just small prizes and recognition, we went from 35 nominations the first time, to 80 nominations the next. The best part for me is reading comments employees make when they cast their votes. They explain why they admire the person and how he or she is inspiring. It not only helps with building the culture, it helps me get to know my employees better."

Performance Management: The Only Tool Most Leaders Have

There is a segment of the business community that wants to get rid of formal performance management, on the charge of being outdated and a waste of time.

No one has convinced us yet. Our opinion is that, yes, bureaucratic performance management practices are a waste of time, but if done right, performance management can be a truly effective tool for managing across functions, units, and geographies. A key benefit of performance management is the opportunities it creates for conversation between leader and employee. It enables greater clarity of focus and better alignment across the organization.

The problem is that many employees, and even many leaders, see performance management processes as rigid, overly formal, and ineffective. They don't realize how powerful a tool it can be when it's applied correctly. It's often the only management tool that a leader is required to use, and we see many managers fall into the bad habit of setting goals that merely enable them to give their employees raises.

However, when management takes this tool seriously and considers what they want to accomplish, creates measurable goals, and manages the accomplishment of those goals, they see a significant improvement in performance and in their bottom lines!

Take for example a start-up technology company we worked with, PayCycle. They had only a few hundred employees. Like any start-up, they were focusing their resources on improving their product and cultivating customer relationships. But every year they made sure to conduct one management training class. The topic: performance management. Why spend their precious time and limited resources on performance management training? They realized it was critical to keep employees focused on achieving key goals.

All the managers, from the CEO down, attended. And the CEO, Jim Heeger, wasn't a 24-year-old Stanford grad. He wasn't there because he had no leadership experience. He was an experienced leader who had worked for companies like Hewlett Packard, Adobe, and Intuit. But he came to learn like everyone else. Heeger came up to us at the end of the program and said, "I have been through many of these classes. But I always learn something. Today I got a new insight into giving feedback that I'll use tomorrow in a tough meeting I have." Jim Heeger understood the power of performance management: He invested in it, trained his leaders in it, and used it.

PayCycle was later acquired by Intuit, at no surprise to us. Not only did they have a great payroll processing product, but they had smart leaders who knew how to create a results-focused organization.

Here is an example of how performance management can yield innovative strategies for growing revenue. It is difficult for a leading publishing house to ignore the shift to e-books. In the last few years sales at one of the big houses were flat, partly because of this shift. After implementing a variety of cost-cutting efficiencies, they realized the next step was to grow revenue.

The senior management team wanted to focus on increasing revenue from books that were already released. Hundreds of new titles are released each year by this publisher. These books are assets that often are underutilized while lots of time and energy and dollars are put into creating and releasing new books. The idea was to figure out how to leverage these hundreds and thousands of assets that, instead of taking up room in a warehouse, could still generate revenue. Each division and department had to come up with their own sub-targets. Then, they were entered into a software program, where the CEO could review what people were aiming for, and more importantly, weekly actions they were taking towards their goals.

One of the unintended consequences was that employees began to work cross-functionally. For example, production discovered that they needed a better understanding of basic finance in order to streamline their processes, so they requested a class on finance for non-finance professionals. An editorial group wanted to better understand marketing so they could tailor their revisions to backlisted products. Innovation and cross-collaboration therefore stemmed from formal performance management procedures.

From SMART to SMA (Short-Term Measurable Action)

Isn't it amazing what we have accomplished as human beings? We have channeled the power of electricity, built huge skyscrapers, and have even put men on the moon! So how did we do it? One thing is certain: We did not do it in one giant step. It took thousands of small steps

RR Recommendation

Make your goals and progress public! Anyone in the world can see the U.S. Patent and Trademark Office's metrics online, in real time, and keep track of the PTO's progress. For example, on the top line in the third circle from the left, they can track the backlog of patent applications. This backlog of patent applications is partially due to the rapid pace of change (new technology, equals new inventions, equals new patent applications). Using this dashboard as a performance management tool, they reduced the backlog from 728,055 to 608,283 within a year after introducing this new "transparency."

Figure 2-3. PTO September 2012 Patents Data-at-a-Glance

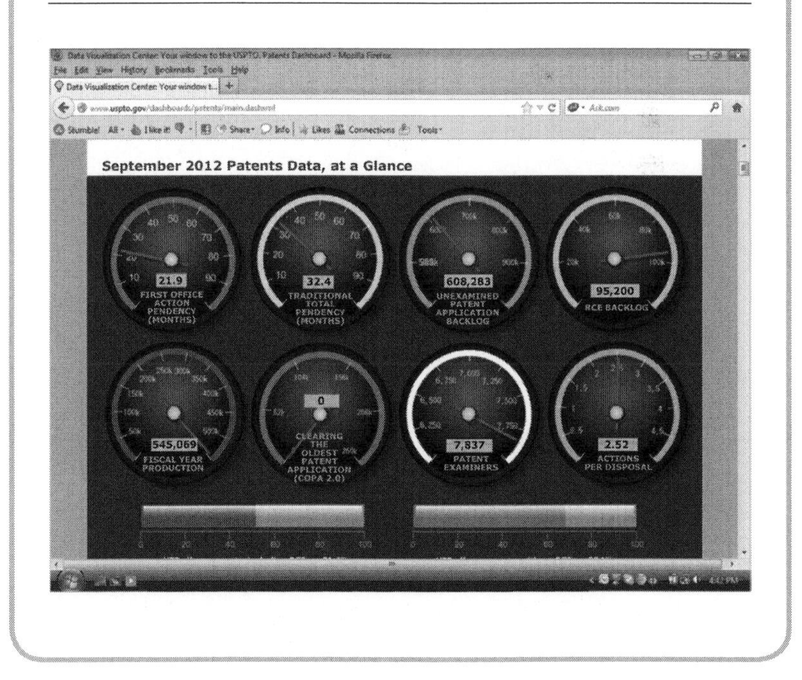

to reach our present level of accomplishment. The accomplishment of short-term goals leads to the achievement of the long-term goal. There is a dynamic relationship between long- and short-term goals.

Rapid retooling is change. And the fact is that change is an emotional business. It causes fear and stress. This is partly due to the fact that it is disorienting. Changes are announced and they seem so big. Often, leaders do not take the time to break it down in sizable chunks.

One way of reducing stress is to break the change down into very short-term, clear objectives. This is the key role of performance management in any rapid retooling situation. Often, S.M.A.R.T. (Specific, Measurable, Attainable, Realistic, Timely) objectives are set for the year, but in two months the environment changes, and those goals don't apply anymore. Short-term goals (though still frequently revisited and updated as overarching goals change) are a much smarter way to manage performance.

Worksheet: SMA Goals

Here are three questions that will help you determine if a goal is "SMA":

- Can it be done in five business days?
- Is it measurable?
- Is it an action?

Example: Assigning an employee to a new job:

- Read your job description by Tuesday. Take note of questions you have, areas you think you will be successful in, and areas you think you will need help with.
- Meet with me on Wednesday to discuss questions and concerns.

It is helpful to meet with your employee and create a few SMAs together when he or she is overwhelmed or seemingly stuck on a big project. The conversation should follow this outline:

- Explain the concept of SMA.
- Provide at least two real examples from your own department or function.
- Create a few SMAs together.
- Follow-up (within a short timeframe) on their progress.
- Offer support and inspiration when they are stuck. Challenge them if they are avoiding taking action.

We are often asked whether yearly *management by objective* (MBO) conversations and yearly goal-setting are still helpful in times of rapid retooling. The answer is "yes!" Many leaders and managers need to be reminded that their employees need direction. Clarity directly affects productivity. Neglecting to frequently revisit organizational objectives and corresponding departmental goals and strategies will certainly lead to confusion, lack of direction, and overworked employees. When things change, it needs to be acknowledged. Objectives should not be frozen in time, but updated as the environment or priorities change.

Chapter 3
Fostering Innovation

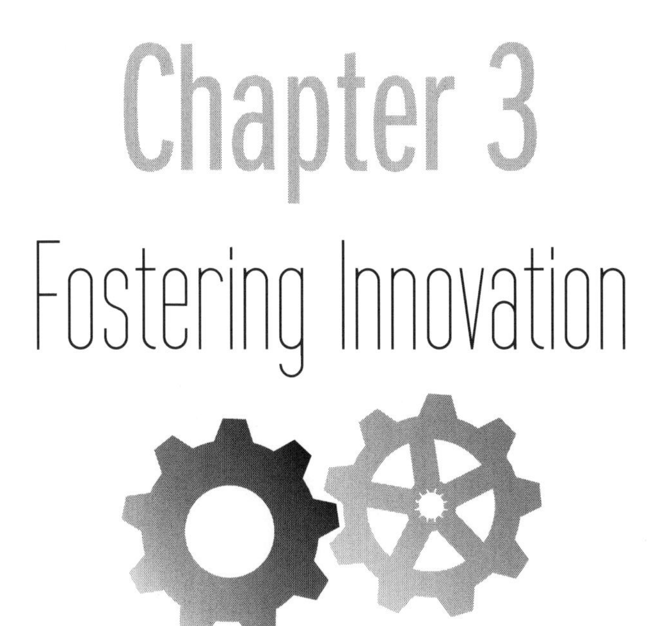

People think of innovation as coming up with and implementing new ideas: new ideas for products, services, finding new markets, new communication approaches, reinventing business processes, and much more. However, if you need to rapidly retool a division or an entire company, innovation is about creating a culture of trust and risk-taking, which enables new ideas to be born and grow. This includes eliminating ideas and attitudes that block innovative thinking and its implementation.

Jamie Gallagher, President and CEO of Faber-Castell USA, says: "Understand that innovation and out-of-the-box thinking is not primarily about creative thinking methods—it's also a way to behave. Assert yourself, dare to fail, and be resilient. Be willing to take risks and try new things and new approaches. The foundation of success across all organizational levels is set by the way you talk to people, assign jobs, and deal with mistakes and failures. To be successful you need first, a vision of who you are (as a company); second, where you are going (as a company); and third, customer understanding and responsiveness."

Know Your Customers

"Creativity for Kids" is the U.S. division that designs craft and activity kits for children that Faber-Castell sells around the world. Gallagher is currently in the middle of focusing on the "ideation" process for the toy-design team in this division. "While we were consistently seeking the input of our retail dealers, our sales team was driving innovation. They would say, 'We need this product, with the following specifications, at this price point, to respond to this customer need.' And they would get their product! Then another need would assert itself and they would do the same thing. It was clear that if we wanted to survive, we couldn't continue to innovate by simply fulfilling retailer requests and competing on price. We had to get back to our market-leader position by understanding the needs of kids and the latest research. We took a step back and reminded ourselves of the importance of creativity for child development. The latest research from the Torrance Tests of Creative Thinking (TTCT) shows us that the divergent thinking and problem-solving capabilities of children have continued to lower in past years. Also diminishing is the hand-mind connection, a skill that is developed by creative playing.

"We wanted to create toys that address the child development needs articulated in this latest research. This also meant that we had to redirect our salespeople. They can't just focus upon a certain price. Salespeople now sit together to prioritize needs as they see them. The ideation team then combines the salespeople's needs with the latest research to lay the groundwork in the design process for a new product.

"We didn't stop there. Currently we are in the middle of cultivating an environment that physically and mentally encourages innovation. We are retooling our creativity center. We are changing the entire workspace—going from cubicles to an open workspace. Also we know the biggest enabler of innovation is *time*. The team has been racing from one request to another. We want to create time to be creative in a focused way. Toy designers need time to spend at schools, playgrounds, museums, children arts places, and so forth, so they can create toys that fit today's child development needs."

Their customer service teams also had to rapidly retool. "Their roles have changed. Customers have become more sophisticated and have more complex needs. This forces organizations to get closer to the customers so that they have a better understanding of them. Today they even attend training sessions conducted by customers (such as Target, Toys R' Us, Michaels, and so forth), or attend trade shows with them; they need to be savvy enough to directly interface the customer's supply chain software. People on the front line now have to make quick decisions based on their business understanding.

"Generally speaking, we are moving from responding to a stream of internal requests, to focusing on external needs—primarily on child development needs as articulated in current research. This approach will enable us to maintain our competitive position as the thought-leader in this field."

Another company that drives innovation based on customer needs is Infragistics. They are a leading-edge user interface design company that services most of the Fortune 500 companies. Infragistics' mission is to develop "killer user interfaces for any browser, platform, or device."

Steve Dadoly is a serial IT entrepreneur and Chief Operating Officer of Infragistics. "With the multitude of technologies available and coming to the market, we live and die by innovation. Our product life cycle is four months! In this environment, the side of the road is littered with great, novel ideas that never made it because there is no customer need." He had to learn this the hard way. Infragistics's solutions were based primarily on Microsoft technology. They waited too long to switch to Apple-based development tools. Thus Infragistics found itself stuck with good products, but with much fewer customers who wanted to buy them. The switch to non-Microsoft development tools eventually happened, but in the meantime they lost revenue.

Dadoly shared with us: "The first thing is to know what the customer wants! If you don't thoroughly know your key customers, don't start any innovation process! Why? Because you risk coming up with wonderful ideas that have little or nothing to do with the business you are in."

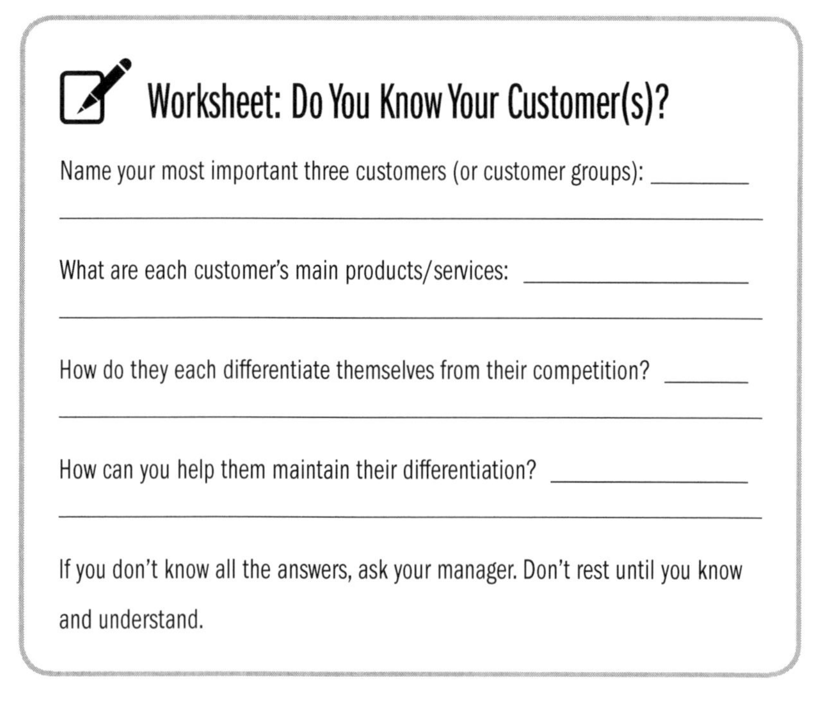

Worksheet: Do You Know Your Customer(s)?

Name your most important three customers (or customer groups): ________

____

What are each customer's main products/services: ________________

____

How do they each differentiate themselves from their competition? ______

____

How can you help them maintain their differentiation? ______________

____

If you don't know all the answers, ask your manager. Don't rest until you know and understand.

RR Recommendation

We recommend you create an index card answering the previous worksheet's questions about each customer of your business or department. Should you be dealing with only internal customers, most questions also apply to them.

- Bring these cards to each meeting. When you are struggling about how to proceed or with a problem that has multiple solutions, pull out the cards and use them to guide you.
- Include these cards during orientation for new employees or interns.
- Hang them in highly visible places—at your water cooler, coffee maker, in your cubicle or your meeting room.

It's worth spending time to reflect on your customers. The most innovative ideas often come from them!

SAP Goes Glocal

SAP (the world leader in enterprise software and software-related services) changed its services to meet the needs of its customer. With economic pressures and the need for organizations to quickly respond to market demands, SAP began offering services in smaller chunks. Instead of having a SAP implementation take up to 24 months, it now offers results through services that can be implemented in only a few months. One of the challenges for employees of SAP in attaining work-life balance is that employees are often assigned to work at their customers' sites for months and years on end, in a different city or state from where they live. Joe Gioffre, a SAP Delivery Executive explains, "Now we provide specific training to specific people to deliver these bite-sized chunks very quickly to customers. This means that employees don't have to remain at the customer site as long.

"We're coining the term 'glocal,' which means using local resources for global reach. For example, I might have folks on the ground in Chicago who have been trained in a service and are close to my customer site, so that travel is not a big issue. But then I might have some specialists who can take on short-term projects who may be based anywhere in the U.S. or abroad. That way you can save on the travel and save on the wear and tear of your consultant, while still providing a very accurate and skilled service to your customers. This also allows us to rotate people to road assignments or home assignments, depending on both their skills and the demands of their personal lives."

This new glocal focus on short-term projects means the company is more nimble in responding to market demands; better able to rapidly retool. For example, just recently they moved 1,000 of their employees to a higher growth area without having to lay off or hire any staff.

Create Trust

Patricia Hill, PhD, Chief Learning Officer at NISC (a national IT services company for the utilities and telecommunication industry), puts it this way: "We need to trust. The traditional command-and-control model does not work anymore. Today's method of developing people in order to get more from them is to build on trust. I have to feel confident that if I offer new ideas, contradict 'common wisdom,' and deviate from the norm, I won't be laughed at. Taking the risk to fail should be rewarded, not ridiculed."

Hill knows this from experience. NISC is a very successful 12-year-old cooperative organization. It is owned by its members who are also its customers. NISC started in 2000, with the merger of two companies with completely different software technologies and architectures. Since that merger, it has created a single enterprise software and architecture, and doubled its employees and member base. Since 2005, it has been annually recognized in Computerworld's Best Place to Work in IT.

In the midst of a very difficult economy, NISC finished its Fiscal Year 2010-11 with the highest revenues in its history and above budget margins. This was spurred by record growth in new membership and accelerated adoption of new technology. How did it do this? Partly with acquisitions; partly by partnering with leading companies, like Lockheed Martin; partly by innovating new technologies to attract and retain members. Its success was built on high levels of trust with all parties involved. To grow and innovate at the pace it did required a culture of flexibility and adaptability, a culture where people were willing to take risks, try new ideas, and challenge "best practices."

We know this is all true because we conducted two employee engagement surveys and associated coaching sessions with Vern Dosch, the CEO, to test if trust levels were where they needed to be. We found its engagement readings were above most companies'.

Trust is key to unlocking the full potential of a team, yet it is so difficult to build and maintain a high trust level in a team. It takes a long time and can be destroyed in a moment. It just takes one wrong comment, being excluded from a single discussion, one instance of not being given credit for an achievement, or the opposite, being wrongly blamed for something. It takes a conscious effort to build trust, it takes time, it takes patience and empathy, and for many of us, puts us in potentially uncomfortable positions where we have to primarily deal with emotions.

For example, the leadership team of an 85-person division was mired in conflict. The new leader was trying to push performance to the next level. The effort was partly driven by her strong, stubborn personality. Partly it was a response to their rapid growth. The scope and pace of the change put a lot of stress and strain on this executive as well as her team.

When we first spoke to her, she told us that the team "wasn't stepping up to the plate," "wasn't taking responsibility for getting things done," and "wasn't offering any new ideas." Our interviews with the team told us they were acting this way because they didn't trust her. She had been pushing them very hard to move forward at a fast pace. In the process, she would lose her patience with them. Sometimes yell. Sometimes insult. This paralyzed the team.

The leader made a fatal mistake. She assumed that her team would automatically buy in to her plans because she was their boss. During times of change, which in this case consisted of both growth and new leadership, her team was waiting to be led, not commanded. The team was not going to offer new ideas because they feared her harsh, public criticism.

Creating a trusting culture is the key to innovation. It creates a safe space for people to make mistakes. It creates the willingness to risk embarrassment, share new ideas, and be wrong in front of management. From these risks, come new ideas.

In our work, we have witnessed a wide range of corporate attitudes toward mistakes. In one of Antoine's first jobs, the CEO and founder of the company (which today is Mettler-Toledo, a leading global balances and scales manufacturer) used to say: "Only people who do not work, don't make mistakes!" What a contrast to a later job Antoine held in "big pharma," when his boss complained bitterly about an email he had

RR Research: The Odds Are Against You

Survey results from PeopleNRG's 2011 and 2012 *Leading Global Change Best Practice Report* showed that the business world in general, particularly in the slower economies, is at an all-time low in trust levels. People feel cheated and robbed by financial systems they don't understand. Additionally, employees are used to endless change initiatives that never produce results. They are announced, begun, and then never fully implemented. Either the leadership changes, the competition changes, or another pressing priority emerges. We call this the *initiative imperative illness*. The illness is a sick desire to create an unmanageable stream of initiatives. As Chris Bear, Director of Sales Training of Prudential Group, explains, "Remember when there were projects? People were assigned to projects. Now there are so many projects, that in the interest of demonstrating the importance of projects, they are called initiatives. Now every month there is a new initiative."

In the face of uncertainty, employees play it safe. They agree to play by the rules of a change initiative, but it is likely that they're not truly onboard with it. Passive aggressive behavior is common in environments of low trust. As a participant in our class once said, "People here deal with change by hiding under the desk and hoping it passes."

sent that included an apology. His boss said: "Never apologize! Then they will think we made a mistake."

The truth is that as you are trying new things, as you are pushing your limits, you will make mistakes. Martin Huber, CFO at Fisba, a high-tech manufacturing company based in St. Gallen, Switzerland,

Worksheet: Trust Checklist

- ☐ I respect my boss, my peers, and employees.
- ☐ I feel respected by them.
- ☐ Our team meetings and conversations are animated.
- ☐ Dissenting views are voiced and discussed.
- ☐ We feel comfortable sharing our insecurities and doubts.
- ☐ I allow myself and others in the team to fail.
- ☐ I take time to make myself understood by people on the team who have a different mother tongue.
- ☐ We allow ample time to address issues and conflicts.
- ☐ We speak with courtesy and respect.

says: "Our company depends on innovation. We succeed by bringing the best high-tech optical device solutions to our customers in the medical, defense, aerospace and other industries. We allow people to make mistakes! Not the same mistake twice of course. But mistakes are part of the learning curve." For example, Fisba has an institutionalized "after-action review" so that top management can review risks they took. They ask themselves after, for example, a reorganization or investing in new production infrastructure, "What did we do right; what did we do wrong?" This only works because there is trust and willingness to acknowledge successes and mistakes. The candid feedback helps them to learn as a team and as individuals.

What better proof of trust than when Fisba employees were willing to take a pay cut during a rough economic time, in order for everyone to keep their jobs. Huber promised that when conditions improved, they would return to their original pay level. After a year, conditions improved and so did their pay, as promised. Huber's vision is that each employee feel like an owner. This example shows that he is achieving his vision. What were some steps he took to get there? The company invests in regular training for employees, which executives are personally involved with. They also prize open communication and ensure that employees understand their business and customers, and are always abreast of the latest developments that affect their industry. This effort to build trust may be the secret of how this manufacturing company has been able to survive in high-price Switzerland.

RR Recommendation

There was a gold standard of sales training when Antoine started his professional career in Switzerland. It was called "Käser Training" (after the name of its inventor). A part of their program was "Blamiere Dich täglich." *Blamiere Dich täglich* is German and means "embarrass yourself daily."

Try it! It will help you to:

- Push your limits.
- Participate when you naturally would not.
- Try new things.
- Have fun.
- Have less fear of making a mistake.
- Raise issues you normally would not raise.
- Ask questions you would normally not ask.
- Experiment when you normally would go the safe route.

A perfect example of allowing mistakes can be seen at Nestlé. After the big success of Nescafé coffee, Nestlé was losing ground in the coffee market in the early '80s. They had become almost insignificant. In attempt to move into a leadership position, they came up with the idea of selling and using coffee in a capsule. However, it took them 10 years of trial and error to perfect it for the marketplace. The initiative started in 1986, but it wasn't until 1995 that they were breaking even. In those nine years there was plenty of opportunity to shelve the idea. But the culture at Nestlé allowed for failure. They had a vision and trusted that eventually it would pay off. The rest is history. Nespresso is now an iconic global high-end coffee brand, with Starbucks (among others) attempting to copy its success formula.

Conflict, Communication, and Innovation

If Steve Jobs read our section above on trust, he'd say, "This is bull!" He did the opposite of instilling trust. He instilled fear. He called employees' ideas stupid. He would openly criticize and insult people's intelligence. And then he would steal their ideas and implement them as if they were his own. Employees at Apple would ask themselves and their colleagues, "What would Steve say about this idea?" This was partly out of fear. The real question in their head was, "What if Steve thinks this idea is stupid and insults me?"

Yet despite this conflict-laden culture, he ended up inspiring innovation and critical thinking. So how can this tyrannical approach to innovation work? Steve Jobs had a vision that was connected to customer needs. He had a remarkably intuitive understanding of what customers would want. (If you don't include his failure with NeXT computers.) And somehow, Steve Jobs and Apple successfully transformed the industry and the way we live.

Steve Jobs is not the only one with this approach. A July 2005 *Harvard Business Review* article, called "Virtuoso Teams," outlined successful teams in the entertainment industry. The big egos competed to get their ideas on their weekly TV shows. They fought hard with each other. This fierce fighting is what drove the success of their shows.

Steve Jobs didn't need a best practice. He didn't need common wisdom. He just went his own crazy way. And it worked for him. But there was a negative side to this kind of conflict. Yes, Apple is the number one market company. But Steve Jobs ruined many relationships on the way to that success, and generated fear, anger, and distrust at the company as well.

We are often asked to coach leaders who create negative conflict but are not, unfortunately, experiencing the success of Steve Jobs. Our four-step process to handle conflict, which we outline in our book *Perfect Phrases for Conflict Resolution*, is:

1. Understand the issue.
2. Envision a solution.
3. Explore alternatives.
4. Agree on action.

We recently worked with a corporate finance department of a multinational industrial conglomerate. As result of a major restructuring that was done to adjust to changing market conditions, corporate finance became more powerful and was expected to develop and enforce a lot of new policies and standards, which were part of the restructuring. The corporate finance people were also charged with creating new accounting and business decision-making tools. To make difficult things more difficult, this restructuring happened during the 2008-09 meltdown. This resulted in a myriad of additional change projects. While the reorganization introduced more direct communication, it had the unexpected effect of creating a lot of resistance from employees. These conflicts made rapid retooling impossible. Things were being delayed for weeks, months, and years. As a result, the regions began asking for the old systems to be reinstituted.

As part of our work with such multinational teams, we interview internal customers to get their perspective. In this case, our interviews with the finance team's partners highlighted several dissatisfactions: communication challenges, lack of buy-in, and a sense of throwing a lot of things over the fence. We reviewed these results with the finance team as part of step one of our conflict process (understand the issue). Even during our meeting, the finance team was defensive and jumping to solutions before clearly understanding the issues at hand. There was a prolonged discussion that didn't relate to the actual issues. So Antoine wrote our four-step process on a slide to guide the team. We had to constantly bring them back to the first step of the process and ask, "What is the issue from the customer point of view?"

It took three hours to explore each of the issues and define their root causes. Then, they prioritized them as high, medium, or low. Once this groundwork was done it became easy to go through the next three steps of the process: agree on a common vision, explore alternatives, and develop actions for the top priorities.

Our experience has taught us that many workplace conflicts may be prevented by taking the time to make sure your ideas are coming across clearly. We call this the IDEA approach, as outlined in the worksheet, *Get Your IDEA Across.*

Conflicts are a major detractor and can dramatically slow down an organization or a team, just opposite to what we want for rapid retooling. We asked a supply chain executive in the above-mentioned

Worksheet: Get Your IDEA Across

Do you have great ideas that nobody is listening to? Take 100 percent of the responsibility for the message being received as intended:

- INTEND: What RESULTS do you want to create?
- DESIGN Message:
    - For whom is it meant?
    - What is the message?
- EXPRESS Message:
    - How will you give your message? In writing? A face-to-face conversation? Other?
    - Openly share your intent and reasoning:
        - "The reason I am telling you this is............."
        - "This is why this is important.........."
- ASSURE Message is received as intended:
    - "What questions do you have?"
    - "Tell me what you think......"
    - "You seem a little (describe their reaction as you perceive it), is that right?"
    - "What is your reaction?"

company about how to compromise when there are conflicting goals. She summed it up well: "You can't come in with a fixed mindset. Show openness and willingness to listen! And make sure they have noticed that you heard them. Then, you'll usually find common ground; particularly if you remind yourselves of the main benefit to the overall company and the customer."

Jamie Gallagher, CEO of Faber-Castell USA, has corporate headquarters in Germany. Are there any conflicts stemming from having owners and executives from another culture and geographic location? Is it preventing rapid retooling? "What helps a lot is if you completely understand the core values and mission and culture of the company. You always have that common ground to get back to. 'Competence and Tradition' are—amongst others—core values of Faber-Castell. You have to know how the organization defines 'competence.' Then it means picking your battles: knowing when to stand up for common values and your organization's interest, and when to let go. Things that are critical to the business need your full attention. Other battles, let them pass."

Institutionalizing Flexibility

We need to be fast, think out of the box, stay ahead of the competition, and at same time be practical and make money. If all of this wasn't already difficult enough, there is one more requirement: You have to make sure your team members are flexible. You may have the perfect foresight, the most innovative ideas and a perfect plan to make them a reality, but if your people are not flexible, you will not succeed. Flexibility is a key ingredient of any rapid retooling environment. How do you foster flexibility amongst your people?

Martin Huber, CFO of Fisba, says, "Flexibility for me means the willingness to contribute personally to process and product improvements, to take another job or to do a job differently, to work more to ensure success. Having a transparent information policy about cost structure is a prerequisite for employee flexibility. Incentives are also important. We encourage improvement suggestions from employees, and if we run with any of the suggestions, we share 50 percent of the initial gains with the person who made it. We also make sure there are immaterial incentives: recognition! And last but not least, flexibility stems from curiosity. Look for people who are curious. People who want to know and understand what happens around them."

Innovation is a developed state of mind. The more you push yourself to be flexible, the more you try to think out of the box, the more innovative you'll be. As Paul Beauchamp, Partner at Deloitte & Touche LLP puts it: "Different people from different cultures will solve the same problem in different ways. By experiencing those differences you allow yourself to consider more options when solving problems yourself."

At PeopleNRG, we have coached many "institutional change agents," at all kinds of organizations. Institutional change agents are full-time employees whose job it is to oversee continual change and growth within their organizations. For example, Pat Hill, PhD, Chief Learning Officer at NISC, explains: "We recently hired a 'technical evangelist.' He has engaged a small, powerful team of technology specialists. They have been challenging our senior team to take new directions, to get into uncharted (technology) territory. So far it has paid off very well. However, we have a retention challenge. How can we create enough new opportunities to keep them busy and excited, while the organization needs the time to process and integrate these new ideas? What seems like rapid retooling to us may seem as very slow retooling to them."

With 250,000 employees, FedEx is using training to help employees be flexible. They rolled out a Quality Driven Management (QDM) program in 2008. Their goal? To turn employees into problem-finders and solution-providers. They want to train employees to not only solve the problem that happened yesterday, but solve the problem that could happen today or tomorrow.

Bob Bennett at FedEx relayed this funny story that demonstrates the goal of QDM. "A courier got a flat tire on his route and he couldn't deliver all his packages that he had to deliver by 10:30. It was a little after 10. So he waves down a UPS driver, transfers his FedEx packages onto the UPS truck. Then he convinces the UPS driver to make his stops first! That's the kind of stuff FedEx is made of."

So far, tens of thousands of FedEx employees have received initial QDM training. Every employee, hourly or salaried, is included because, as Bennett says, "They are all important to building our future."

At IBM, "We have had ongoing transformation since Gerstner was in charge in the 90s, responding to the changing economy, doing more with less, and growing oversees employees and customers," says Jim Carey, Learning Manager at IBM. Carey works with his team to support business transformation within IBM. "We are now starting to look at how to transform systematically. Our leaders know that the people who respond to the growth markets the fastest will be the winners. Our job is to support the continual transformation of our business to help IBM win."

Carey continued, "Traditionally, employees are seen as the targets of change. They are seen as resistant to the changes being pushed by leaders. But actually, employees are stakeholders in and not targets of the change. They want to be a part of creating the change; they want their voices heard. Our team's job is to teach employees how to participate in change and be a driver of change, rather than just complaining through a survey or an employee focus group. If you want to be a partner in deciding and co-creating change, you have to think systematically about change management. We are teaching employees methods to solve problems. During training, we have them apply the methods and tools to real challenges, so employees get practice in recommending solutions based on analysis. Leaders then review the employee ideas and, if approved, the employees implement the solution. The employees are then the real change agents."

De-Tooling to Retool

Franz Aatz, venture capitalist and "serial-entrepreneur," reminded us of an often-overlooked truth: "The biggest challenge may not be retooling but 'de-tooling'! Before going to the 'new' it may be a good idea to critically review the old. You need to let go of old ideas to be able to clear your head for new ideas." He continued, "We are often enamored of 'best' practices, but be aware, they are often in the way of 'new' practices. Best practices are about documenting what worked in the past. Innovation often means rethinking best practices and experimenting with new practices!"

Aatz says: "What I also learned is that each time your company reaches a new milestone, many employees have to start from the beginning, again and again, to reorient themselves. A lot needs to be thrown overboard, and we need to behave as if we were new to the business. A lot of what was learned so far is not only irrelevant now, but very likely is counter-productive! De-tooling is crucial for rapidly growing companies. We now need a lot of openness, trust, willingness to fail, to take controlled risk. If people are closing their doors and saying there is nothing they can do, I know that either I have the wrong people or I am not doing enough to change their attitudes."

Worksheet: De-Tooling

- Do you have any "best practices," golden rules, standard operating processes? What are they?

___

___

___

- Which ones are getting in the way of progress?

___

___

___

- What can YOU do about it?

___

___

___

Innovation Tips and Tools

Much of the premise of our book is that there is a need to be able to adjust "just in time." However, in some industries or situations, this is not enough. Rapid retooling also means to constantly think ahead: "What will it look like once we turn this corner? When we have reached this milestone?" Otherwise, we don't know what we don't know.

Companies sometimes feel restrained by limited budgets for traditional "research and development." However, innovation doesn't always need a generous R&D budget. It can happen anywhere, anytime. All employees are potential innovators. This is why small companies, with smaller R&D budgets, are not at a disadvantage. Rather, their processes, approaches, and decision-making protocol are often less ingrained. This means there is more room for experimenting and trying new things.

We asked Dr. Daniel Pascheles, Vice President, Head of Global Competitive Intelligence at Merck, how he was innovating. "I ask my folks to come up with at least two or three new ideas as part of the objective-setting process each year. We have to find new ways of creating value. We need to know the pressure points of our industry and its environment to constantly be ahead of the game. And in order to do so and to add value for our internal customers, we have to constantly show them how rapidly the world changes and what new opportunities (and threats) such a changing world is offering."

Pascheles has implemented a simple and systematic innovation process for his team of 20 people who operate around the globe. At the beginning of the year they meet for a two- to three-day workshop where they do a few things:

- Look back on what happened last year—what worked well, where could they have done better.
- Introduce a topic of research, latest best practice, or new thought leadership.
- Define their stretch objectives as a team and link them to their long-range plan (for the next three or four years).

An important part of this objective-setting process is that each of Pascheles's team members has to identify three innovation objectives. Thus, as part of their standard goal-setting process, the team is tracking 60(!) individual innovation objectives each year, some of them small, some of them big.

Pascheles says, "The web has changed the rules of the market. In our case, online pharmacies suddenly sprouted up. An objective of one employee involved looking at this change and figuring out how to adapt to it. It's something the traditional pharma companies first did not want to touch. It was an unregulated space and accordingly hard to get a handle on. But Merck felt it had a responsibility to protect its patients, and that these distribution channels outside the regulatory space were worth investigating. So, as a result of this employee's innovation goal, we started to build a database and to research web-based pharmacies. We now know that out of the 10,000 online pharmacies, 9,800 are not complying with our standards. When you search for pharmaceutical products online, 98 percent of the offers lead you to websites that sell medication, which is not authentic. This problem is now a major topic being addressed by the regulatory agencies in Washington, D.C. (and around the globe)."

This one employee goal made Merck a knowledge expert in this area: a company which understands the market and understands the risks to users of medication. This gave them credibility with their customers, with colleagues at conferences, and the regulatory agencies.

This example shows how, when leaders set employees loose to innovate and support their work, one employee can have a huge impact on a company and its industry. Another tool Pascheles uses is "the white sheet of paper approach." With it, he is encouraging his employees to block all the distractions in the corporate system, and let them turn it upside down if they want to (and have the courage to!). "I give them a blank sheet of paper and say: 'No restraints. If you could (re-) define the work that you currently do, how would you do it? What would you need to be successful?' It's funny; it sometimes feels as if I have to teach them that nobody gets fired for doing something that makes business sense. 'We've never done it this way' is not a good argument! I believe that anybody can change anything. You don't have to wait—the company has to change. That's the only way it will continue to be successful. And it all starts with a white sheet of paper, and no limitations!"

Stavros Michailidis says that daily problem-solving at work provides practical opportunities for innovation. He is the founder of Innovation Bound, a firm that consults to Fortune 500 companies, academic institutions, government agencies, and NGOs to create valuable thought leadership, reinvent their organizations, launch new ideas, and solve complex problems.

"Much of the value leaders add at work is problem solving. They can add even more value if they take a new look at their problem-solving approach. Problem solving has four unique and distinct phases. Each of these phases provides an opportunity for innovation."

Lukas Elmiger, the COO of MacxRed, says "Rapid retooling means modularization! You have to bring structure to a problem. Break it up into steps; divvy up the work leading to the solution. Reduce complexity!"

In this spirit, MacxRed introduced a facilitated process to support innovation. When they have a new idea, they bring in someone from the company who does not understand the specific solution or problem. He or she acts as a facilitator, asking questions until she understands the situation, using this template:

1. Summarize the idea.
2. Why are we doing this (background, bases of research, context)?
3. What are the elements of the solution?
4. What do our historic experiences tell us about this current problem and the suggested solution?

5. How could we make it a success?
6. How long will it take? How can we accelerate it?
7. How do we measure success?

MacxRed also leverages other companies in its industry. There is a rapidly growing software development community, which is building and sharing its applications with public domain sites. Many software developers don't want to exclusively rely on knowledge and skills components within their companies anymore. "This dramatically accelerates our execution and reduces risks of errors by leveraging other people's code and other people's experiences."

Felix Wenger, Managing Director, UBS (one of the world's leading banks), explains how UBS uses incremental innovation to mitigate risk. "Customer interaction patterns have been changing at a very rapid pace. Through the availability and use of 'new media channels' such as social networking platforms, a lot of the marketing responsibility has transitioned from a centralized marketing department to individual (customer-facing) employees. Every one of these employees becomes a potential innovator. Many are experimenting with new media, as they want to access their customers through the customers' preferred channel. And of course they always strive to find access to new customers and new potential customer groups.

"This innovation comes with risk, a lot of work, and resistance! A major role of our corporate office is to mitigate the risk. As you know, banking is a highly regulated industry, anytime you are doing anything new; you need to check with legal and compliance. Often you have to write new policies and define new standards. So in e-media, each time an employee works on a new project, we help him or her to work out the compliance and regulatory issues. We have introduced an

Worksheet: 4 Ways to Innovate While You Problem Solve

1. Clarify the problem. The opportunity here is to reframe the problem—instead of simply clarifying the situation, find new ways to interpret the issue. Seek unique perspectives from those who don't embrace the common understanding of the problem. What are new ways to look at this problem?

2. Find one or more solutions. The opportunity is to stop looking for the right answer and start looking for lots of interesting options. Think about it: If you find the most obvious and straightforward answer you are pretty much guaranteed to get the most common results. If you are really after innovation you must look for a different type of solution. What are some interesting options?

3. Plan the solution. The opportunity is to enhance the plan. Two companies can pursue essentially the same idea, with vastly different approaches (think *Encarta* vs. *Wikipedia*). Innovation isn't just about what we're doing, it's also about how we do things. What new approaches can generate new types of results?

____

____

____

____

____

____

4. Execute the solution. The opportunity is to improvise during implementation. Planning is a valuable process, but we must remain open to change as we execute the plan. Along the way we will face unforeseen obstacles and gain new insights. Remain flexible and adaptive during implementation. Be open to stumbling upon "new value" by continuously learning from the implementation processes' successes and failures. Where can you improvise?

____

____

____

____

____

____

____

Content contributed by Stavros Michailidis. Printed with his permission.

E-Channel Center of Excellence approach as a change-management and risk-reduction strategy.

"Each rollout is regional and thematically limited, not global. To facilitate rapid retooling within the organization we need to ensure positive experiences for the employees who initiate change. After the first success with an idea, other areas may want to do the same. They can build on the initial experience and move in a 'safer space' as all of the compliance and regulatory work has already been taken care of.

"People are very interested in using our service. Currently we work with a group that focuses on philanthropy and wants to create a philanthropic social network. They are establishing a more permanent communication with people who, previously, they would have only met once a year at a conference. Another example is an advertising initiative proposed by a group: buying 20,000 email addresses of potential new customers within a certain age group who use social media as their main way of communicating with family, friends, and colleagues. We are learning a lot with each project. It's a perfect win/win for both parties—corporate and the field operation. Our only problem: So far we have only reached the early innovators—a minority of maybe 20 percent. Our big question now is how to reach and entice more people to build on these early successes and become innovators themselves."

Innovation and rapid retooling are prerequisites to survival. If Nokia had systemically applied rapid retooling, would they be in the situation they are today? Same with Dell or American Airlines. IBM did, and is experiencing success. Yet Compaq and Digital Equipment don't exist anymore. Urgency and survival instinct are often the impetus for rapid retooling. Make sure you don't wait too long to innovate!

Chapter 4

Overcoming Silo Thinking

Innovation and silo-busting are inextricably connected in today's fast-paced business world. An organization cannot expect to compete without breaking down silos. In this chapter you learn how to become a relationship management champion and "silo buster." We live in a world of social networks, permanent reachability, and easy travel, and yet establishing trustful, productive relationships has become more and more of a challenge. Those new tools and technologies do not automatically eliminate boundaries. Although communication has technically become faster and easier, the risk of miscommunication has grown dramatically. Boundaries become even more pronounced and the "walls" between departments even bigger, an ideal breeding ground for misunderstandings. The result: Silos are well and alive!

Get People Together

There are a lot of people who have an interest in maintaining silos, as they are a way to maintain an area of influence or to protect their own turf. It all starts at the top: If top executives can't come together and align their goals to the good of the company, if they communicate ambiguously and don't "walk the talk," the organization at large will feel the effects of that behavior and emulate it.

We have had people in our workshops who have been working in the same corporate headquarters for years; in the same building, on the same floor, separated only by a few yards—but had never met each other until they came to our workshop. Another perpetual complaint we hear is, "Why are my colleagues sending me emails when they work just a few cubicles away? It would be so much easier (and healthier!) if they just walked down the hall and talked to me!" Does any of this sound familiar to you? How do you overcome these "physical" boundaries?

RR Recommendation

Amanda Parsons, Deputy Commissioner at the New York City Department of Health: "Every month my executive team meets as a team and then with my boss, Health Commissioner Thomas A. Farley. It breaks down silos across my team if they have to all meet with my boss." Getting functions to meet and work together on solving problems is the first step to breaking down silos.

Siloes don't naturally crumble over time. You have to create opportunities to get people together. Sergio, the CEO of a global financial organization, stresses the importance of *horizontal governance*. His rapid retooling efforts focus on eliminating anything that causes delays and slows down decision making. Historically his organization has operated very bureaucratically, and is fragmented across many constituencies, which differ in language, culture, national particularities, and so forth. This created a very slow and very "siloed" organization. "Nature is divisive; people just see their own little piece. To correct this we needed to enable people to see our goals and processes holistically. That is why we implemented horizontal governance. It allows us to understand business urgency across horizontal boundaries. Regular meetings are very helpful. For example, we introduced periodic policy meetings for senior staff."

Sergio further explains how this approach was important in reaching middle management. They created special forums every month for middle managers to collaboratively identify any silo-related problems, conduct planning and performance review exercises, discuss cross-functional issues and come up with solutions, and then communicate back to their superiors and constituencies. Does this all sound obvious to you? Sometimes it doesn't take a sophisticated solution, but the discipline to implement simple ones!

We also really enjoyed Sergio's advice on how to communicate better across organizational divides and get buy-in from stakeholders. "Don't just take one approach! Try everything: Some people respond to technical benefits of a plan, some to personal, some to political pressure, and so forth. We do it any way we can. There are just two things we can't do when rapidly retooling: second-guess ourselves and become discouraged over what seems like a painfully slow process."

Make-A-Wish International is a nonprofit, represented in nearly 50 countries around the globe by its 37 affiliate offices. It operates separately from Make-A-Wish America and is currently focused on creating the same successes—notoriety and brand awareness in particular—as its American counterpart, only through a dramatically more fragmented global context. To do this, they have to be able to adjust to the needs and the personalities of each country. As much as each wish of their children is different, so are many of their campaigns around the globe. The competitive charitable climate is one they must be aware of and innovative enough to withstand, and hopefully overcome. Without the ability to rapidly and flexibly adapt to ever-changing needs and implement lessons learned from one country to the other, they would not be the successful organization they are today. It is through that success that the courageous children they serve have the opportunity to experience the granting of their wishes.

A key approach they use to foster cross-functional and cross-regional thinking is through CEO-level regional roundtables. Launched in April 2012, this approach has provided the means to facilitate quick learning across the globe. Make-A-Wish International has implemented three regional round tables (two days in length, once a year), one each for Asia, Latin America, and Europe.

All CEOs, as well as applicable staff and volunteers of these regions, are invited to this two-day event, which is later followed up by virtual meetings. Each roundtable is focused on a different topic, and is tailored to the needs of the CEOs through the simple action of reaching out to them ahead of time with a short survey. This produces a list of topic ideas, of which the group is then asked to identify the five most important. The CEOs receive an invitation with a request to come prepared to discuss challenges, successes, and best practices relative to the chosen topics. The meeting begins with an overview of the topics, and then follows with an open discussion format, according to the passions and urgencies demonstrated by the CEOs and attendees. It encourages innovative problem solving.

After the in-person discussion has been completed, one-hour webinars are scheduled and held to continue the conversation and address any topics that may not have been addressed. In addition, the meeting allows for the tracking of action items determined at the in-person meetings. Elizabeth Greene, Director of Organizational Learning at Make-A-Wish International, says "My communication advice, especially when working in a critical timeline, is to closely observe body language cues and listen. Email robs us of many rapid reaction opportunities. I'm Skyping affiliates as often as possible. In my global environment it is invaluable to see their body language and to be able to make a personal connection. A Skype conversation is more immediate. It is easier to capture spontaneous reactions and honest opinions. It's a wonderful tool for focused, accelerated problem resolutions and for building commitment. At the same time we all need to occasionally step away from any given task for a moment and understand why we are doing this task and how it relates to the bigger picture for the team, the organization, the community, and the world!"

Common Goals Make or Break Silos

As mentioned earlier, common objectives are key to reducing silos and accelerating retooling. Many of our consulting experiences show that when team leaders and executives clarify the organization's direction, it becomes easier for employees to adapt and reorient themselves at any given moment. Common objectives are like road signs. They help us navigate uncharted territory.

We once worked with a global leadership team in Russia whose leader was disturbed by the fact that none of the team members took ownership of the organizational goals. This limited their capacity to respond to the many opportunities in their quickly growing market.

While interviewing the team it became clear that the executive had never communicated the team objectives. Every member had clearly-defined individual, functional objectives, but they were never discussed with each other and no attempts were made to align them with the team's overarching goals. And as so often is the case when there is no alignment at the top, the misalignment is amplified as you go down the organizational ladder. It weakened the team's productivity, and had a very negative impact on its organizational flexibility and adaptability.

So what we did was:

- Clarify the leadership team objectives with the team leader, then communicated them to his team.
- Align personal goals of individual team members with the overall objectives.

After their next meeting, the leader sent us a note saying, "We just had the most productive team meeting ever!" Why? Defining and aligning the team objectives and knowing how to help each other went a long way towards creating a new spirit of ownership and collaboration.

In a follow-up conversation, another regional executive in the organization concurred: "Explaining overall targets and common goals is invaluable. Make sure you take the necessary time to do this. It has been surprising for me how much key stakeholders have been willing to accommodate those overarching goals once they understood them. The combination of clarifying goals and presenting facts as they evolve are very powerful rapid retooling tools!"

Vala Afshar also knows about silo-busting. As Chief Customer Officer at Enterasys Networks, he is responsible for worldwide services operations and technical support functions, including contact center operations, field engineering, support engineering, and infrastructure technologies.

Collaboration at Enterasys was not always the way it is now. When a private equity team took ownership of the company, the new CEO said they had to "fix the company." He came up with a new tagline: "Nothing is more important than the customer." It sounded nice, but it would require a lot of changes to the organization's current processes to make his vision a reality.

Afshar says, "For us, retooling was the notion of shared accountability. The account executive is the CEO for the customer—if the field calls, he has to deliver on his promise to the customer. We use SalesForce.com to manage our business and display balanced performance scorecards for each function. As an example, when a customer contacts our call center, the system automatically notifies the account representative solutions engineer, as well as the sales team responsible for that customer. So immediately the services function is engaged with the sales function, and both are aware that the customer just contacted the support center. Based on the severity of the case, it's up to the account executive to determine if he or she wants to intervene or whether they want to delegate it to customer service. This instantaneous communication and collaboration helps us achieve a 70 percent resolution of customer service problems during the first call. For a hardware company our size, the typical rate for first contact closure is around 50 percent. So 70 percent is actually very, very good."

Afshar also actively develops employee business acumen and uses performance management tools. "We share dashboards and individual and departmental performance goals. We can do this by region or larger geographies, or down to the account executive level. We have quarterly business reviews and monthly cross-functional meetings, in which different lines of business discuss their performance collectively. All the performance metrics are designed according to the business strategy for growth as the entire organization understands it. This enables us to act quickly and respond in unison to new issues that come up."

Building an Integrative Structure

As Steve Dadoly, COO at Infragistics, says, "When a company is growing, so are the number of silos." Often, once a company goes global, the silos are made of individual countries. A global Europe-based manufacturing company had this situation. They were very successful and experiencing a strong growth curve. One of the success factors during this growth had been to let each local (country-based) entity operate on its own to maximize profit. This led to a very siloed organization. Those geographical entities were managed with a very entrepreneurial spirit; they had a high degree of autonomy, and sometimes would even compete with each other for business. This competition worked to a point. However, as growth started to slow, and external competition became stronger, the executive board realized that it had to introduce a new approach. They needed a globally-aligned strategy, an increased capability to move quickly on a global scale, and a focus on profitable growth for the consolidated companies. So what did they do? They created a matrix structure, consolidating countries in larger regional entities and creating functional and marketing-based corporate competence. This not only enabled them to compete more effectively, but it allowed them to quickly react to a dramatically changing global business environment (triggered partially by the 2008-09 banking crisis and its ripple effects). Less hierarchical levels, easier access to expertise, and more holistic decision making helped them to:

- Optimize access to credit globally.
- Cut redundant projects across locations.
- Manage stock levels globally.
- Collectively use purchasing power globally to get better prices from suppliers.
- Optimize staffing across regions.

There is, however, a caveat to the matrix approach: It creates access at the price of complexity. The clear, simple hierarchies are replaced by multiple reporting lines, which often contribute to confusion. And as the matrix seems less entrepreneurial there is a risk of silo building, which would be exactly what the matrix organization would like to prevent. This needs to be carefully watched to make sure the matrix is a facilitator of rapid retooling and not an impediment to it. The way to do it, as documented above, is to communicate and foster understanding of common goals and progress. And don't miss any opportunity to celebrate. Celebrate success; show how it was achieved through a collective effort. This builds a winning team!

The lattice organization takes the matrix one step further in flexibility. It enables organizations to adapt to shifting customer needs by shifting their own resources more readily. Instead of managers, employees are assigned as needed to projects, with coaches (not supervisors) who help them succeed. Budgets are not assigned to departments, but are developed as needs arise by senior people (or anyone really), who make a case for the project and secure financial buy-in.

This lattice concept is what NISC implemented. They wanted to be much faster in responding to changing customer needs and create a product and services portfolio, which would allow them to develop new products more swiftly and at the same time reduce maintenance cost of the existing products. In a lattice structure, opportunities for learning and advancement come not just from moving up in the organization, but from moving laterally to new technologies and projects. Leaders and managers take on the role of a coach (which puts some managers out of their comfort zones). However, this structure is designed to destroy silos, integrate product lines, and combine multiple divisions. Pat Hill, PhD, Chief Learning Officer at NISC, told us that the lattice structure is improving flexibility to respond to customer demands, more easily assigning resources to projects, and increasing employee learning, growth, and retention.

BMW Manufacturing made more simple structural changes to help them respond to market changes. To the benefit of the consumer, auto makers are always focused on innovation. Werner Eikenbusch, Manager of Apprenticeship and Associate Training at BMW's U.S. factory, explained: "We are always focused on improving. We have internal quality targets that drive our innovation, but then you also have external factors, like J.D. Power, evaluating us. The competition is also moving us along. If you see that everybody else is improving at a certain pace, you don't want to fall behind—you want to overtake them. So the speed of improvement becomes a big discussion topic."

The pace of innovation was reaching a plateau at the BMW plant. Werner told us, "In the U.S., the impetus was ultimately given by the president of BMW's U.S.-based manufacturing plant, Josef Kerscher. He tasked the vice presidents of quality, engineering, and production with coming together to figure out what they could do to accelerate the pace of improvement. They felt that the question was really, what else can we do? We've done so many different things, what *else* can we do? That was the point when they began to consider the 'rapid retooling' approach.

"What they realized was that they had to break up all of the silos. You have to bring people together and have them work together. For example, offices were grouped by function. Engineering sat together, logistics sat together, and so forth. Functions even ate together. So what we did was to change office assignments. Each function had a representative move near the production line. Let's assume I have eight planners and each planner supports one portion of the production line. Instead of the eight planners sitting together, each planner now sits with a production person. So now you had a cross-functional team sitting together. They started to have common meetings in which they would discuss issues. They would talk about their targets across departmental boundaries. It's really all about teamwork, decentralizing, and working together."

However, they had some kinks to work out. "We are a very target-oriented company. When we introduced this cross-functional approach, it became clear (particularly when conducting focus groups) that everybody was thinking, 'Yes, that all sounds great, but at the end of the day, who's going to evaluate my performance? If supporting this production team is not on my target sheet or my supervisor doesn't care about it, then ultimately, I can't really be held accountable because I'll be evaluated against different standards.' We realized this was going to be a big obstacle to cross-functional collaboration. So we said, okay, we need to work on getting agreement on some basic targets for which everybody will be jointly responsible. After we had agreed on those baseline targets, managers from all the different groups signed off on them and agreed to be held accountable to support the targets."

Unfortunately, changing employees' seats alone doesn't always work. In an effort to save money in the midst of a New York City fiscal crisis, the NYC Department of Health made a very large physical move. For years, their 6,000 employees were spread throughout out the five boroughs. Some worked in city-owned buildings, others in leased spaces. As everyone knows, real estate is at a premium in NYC. They decided to consolidate 4,000 employees into a new building in Long Island City (just a few minutes from Manhattan over the East River). They also hoped that the new location, which had open-space cubicles, would foster greater collaboration.

In fact, the move did not by itself foster collaboration. Amanda Parsons, Deputy Commissioner at the NYC Health Department, told us, "Before we consolidated locations, we lost a lot in terms of cross-fertilization. We were in all different buildings and it was really difficult to get everybody in a room for a discussion. However, I was amazed that putting people in the same building did not reduce a lot of silos. On some floors, one bureau takes up one row, and the next row of cubicles is another bureau. But no one knows the names of the people across the aisle! So for areas that don't work together but sit near each other, we are using an approach that worked in my previous bureau—organizing informal activities to get to know each other."

Once again, Apple is the exception to the rule. They appear to *set up* silos. The iPod people work with the iPod people. The iPhone people work with the iPhone people. In fact, they can't even access each other's office buildings. This highlights a key element of silo busting:

You don't break down silos just to break them down. You get people together who need to be together for business reasons. Apple creates collaboration by building teams that have all the people and resources they need to succeed.

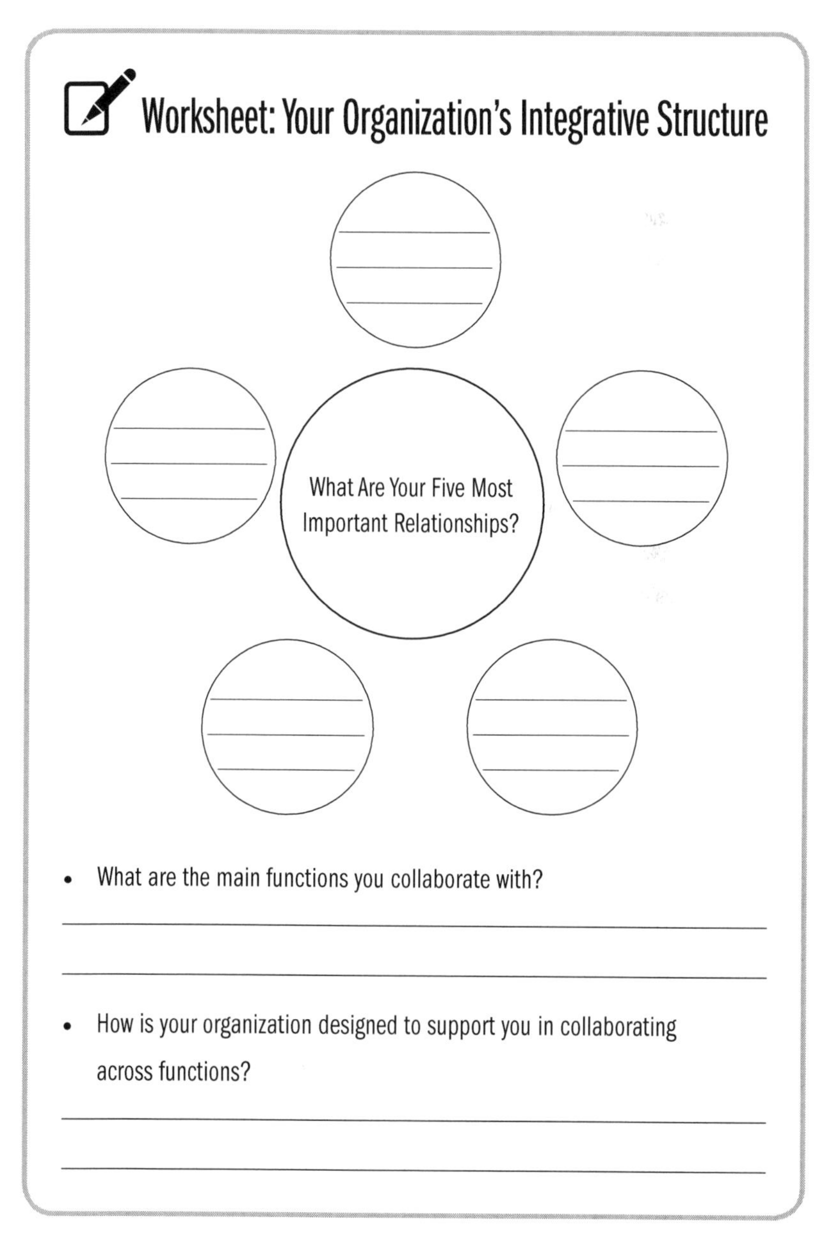

Worksheet: Your Organization's Integrative Structure

What Are Your Five Most Important Relationships?

- What are the main functions you collaborate with?

____

____

- How is your organization designed to support you in collaborating across functions?

____

____

Building Rapid Relationships

The core service of consulting firms is rapid retooling. The consultants' job is to retool their client organizations in any given area. And because consultants are working with a constant stream of new faces (as well as new initiatives), they have to constantly build new relationships. Consulting firms have known for a long time that building relationships across boundaries is not only good for *their* business, but also their clients'!

Worksheet: Building Rapid Relationships

What do people in your organization do...

...to build or improve relationships quickly? ______________________

____

...to damage relationships quickly? ______________________

____

John Morgan, a telecommunication expert working for a leading global consulting organization, stresses the importance of establishing a personal relationship before diving into a business project: "Unless you establish a relationship with the people you're dealing with, they may feel like you're there with an agenda, you're there to tell them what their issues are, or that you're putting your agenda on their agenda."

This is something to keep in mind even if you are not a consultant. Business relationships are assets. Not only to your external customer development, but also with each of your internal customers and peers. You want to shore up your "relationship capital." This way you can dip into these human resources when you need them. Your relationship capital critically affects your ability to rapidly retool.

How do you establish good customer relationships, both internally and externally? John Morgan says, "As a consultant all I have is influence. My typical project length is only a few weeks or months, and during this time I have to revamp a department or an entire company. The only real tool I have to accomplish this is my ability to influence people. So the goal of a first meeting with my clients should not be plowing through the 10 items on my agenda, but finding common ground with the people I am trying to work with.

"I know that what I'm going to tell you is nothing new, but I'll mention it anyway. Because in our task-oriented, overloaded, rapid world we run the risk of forgetting it. Find some ways to connect with your new partner. What interests do they have? What is on their desk? Listen for offhand comments that shed light on their personal lives. If you don't establish this kind of personal connection, then when it is time to get fast results, you'll find that you have a more difficult time persuading or motivating your client. People are always more willing to share and collaborate once there is genuine trust, respect, and friendliness."

How Do I Say This?

There is always a balance to strike between the value of face-to-face dialogue, and the cost-value of saving on travel and time away from the office. In a perfect world we'd have all critical or complex conversations face to face. Not the least because when we are face to face, most of us usually try to get results and keep the peace. When communicating via email or another method of written communication, it is easier for people to sink into disagreements or create misunderstandings.

RR Research: Leadership in Unlikely Places

PeopleNRG conducts a yearly global survey investigating trends in change leadership around the globe. It consists of 18 questions, answered by 550 professionals from close to 50 countries. The graphics below depict the 2011 and 2012 results. We found that during times of change people will trust influential non-leaders—employees who are not official leaders within the organization, but who are seen as valuable resources and trusted and respected by their peers. During ambiguous times people look to those they can rely on for information and direction. Which is why, no matter what your role in an organization, it is important to nourish and maintain strong relationships of trust across your organization—you'll have more willing, supportive, and savvy partners during times of change.

Figure 4-1. Trust Levels in Informal Leaders During Change

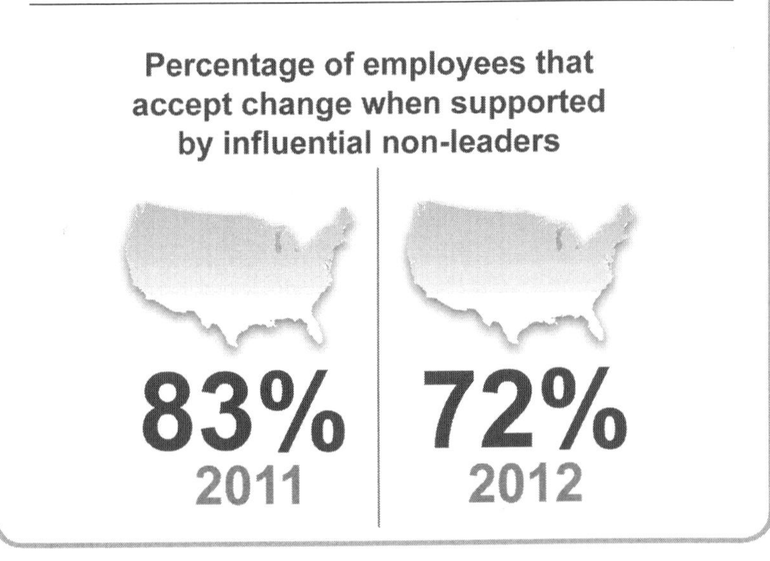

However, the reality is that we can't always travel. Video conferencing is a good "stop gap" to this problem. It is more and more affordable and available. With Skype, iPhone Face Time, and video capability built into WebEx, GotoWebinar, AT&T Connect, and Adobe Connect, you have powerful "silo-breaking" (or at least "silo-weakening") tools at your fingertips.

The problem many of us run into is overusing email, especially when communicating globally. Clients often tell us how inadequate of a communication tool email can be. While it can be very efficient for some communication tasks, it can be useless or even dangerous in other communication situations. That is why we put together a tool to help you decide when to use email versus when to use more multidimensional methods such as phone and video.

Figure 4-2. Deciding on a Communication Method

ONE DIMENSIONAL

MULTI-DIMENSIONAL

Email
Chat
Blog

Phone

Web Meeting

Video Conference

Face to Face

Factors to Consider	One Dimensional Media	Multi Dimensional Media
Content	Fact Simple Familiar Low Priority	Emotional Complicated Unfamiliar Urgent
Interaction	None Inform	Discuss Influence Innovate
Relationship	Strong Time Tested	Weak New Need to Address Conflict or Relationship Issue
Location	Different Time Zone	Nearby Same Time Zone
Cultural Factors	Be aware of your audience	

The Importance of Reaching Across Cultural Divides

Erick Hoversholm, Planner and Operations Officer for the U.S. Army, told us this story about when he was recently stationed in Afghanistan. It is a wonderful example of how simple it can be to break down silos.

There was a group of five locals who lived right outside the gate of the Army compound. They would greet the Americans in the Afghani way: They'd bow or put their hand across their chests to say hello. At first Erick didn't know how to respond, but soon he started to mimic their gestures. This was met with appreciation. Erick said, "I would try to use words and gestures and they would laugh. But then they were more willing to work with me. They enjoyed watching us stumble through. When I left for R&R, this one guy was really upset and seemed to miss me. Before I left he came up to me and said 'Thank you very much' and shook my hand." This was a completely foreign ritual for him. But he was now trying to learn my customs and reach out to me. This one moment deepened my level of respect for and appreciation of these people with whom I interacted every day."

Putting It All Together

Busting silos should also be the result of deploying the ideas from our previous chapters: building business acumen, and creating a culture of trust and communication. In his former role as COO and SVP of the Retirement Services division at American Express (a $200 million global operating unit with 1,500 employees), John Baker's employees had strong business acumen, they were innovative, and silos weren't an issue. He ran a profitable business that sold financial services to Fortune 500 companies. But one day he and his executive team, after returning from a successful three-day strategy session with top executives from every region of the country, got a disturbing phone call. In essence he was told, "Beginning Monday, you are no longer an American Express division—we don't know what your brand will be, we don't know what your technology will be or what you should tell your customers. All we can tell you is that your division is being sold."

"From that point on," Baker says, "I had the privilege to witness extraordinary employee passion and uncompromising commitment in the face of cataclysmic change. Our executive team figured that one-third of our employees would lose their jobs, one-third would be retained by American Express, and one-third would be hired by the acquiring firm, but not one employee knew which bucket he would ultimately fall into. Complicating the issue, we had to deal with extremely aggressive competitors actively trying to poach both clients and employees, and anxious clients exhausted with the roiling marketplace and seeking stable service partners. But despite our gloomy predictions, we managed to retain 90 percent of employees and deliver over 93 percent client retention during the transition period."

So how did he do it? First, they already had processes in place that developed the business acumen of their employees. "On day two of our new employee orientation, we went over in detail how we made money. We reviewed our P&L. We showed employees how a prospect turned into a client and how we serviced them so that we can generate a profit. We even showed margins. They knew from the start how we made money and exactly how their role contributed to expense or profit. So when we announced these changes, they understood it wasn't personal. We explained the competitive analysis so they knew what we were facing as a business. They understood the business dynamics because we were always talking openly about the business dynamics."

On top of this, Baker and his team had shaped a culture of trust. "We had a policy to tell people what we knew when we knew it. Whether we had bad quarters or good, we shared it. When we lost a bid, we shared it and conducted a brutally honest review of why we lost it. This wasn't to assign blame, but so we could know exactly what needed to improve. Our communication was truthful and timely of both good news and bad." If you are not candid with the people you are leading, then when times are rough you can't have their trust. When this crisis hit, Baker's employees believed him when he explained the situation. "We explained the three buckets they could end up in (job loss, transfer, or retention) and we told them as soon as we knew they'd know. And because we'd been through times like this in the past, they trusted us."

He also helped his leaders become good communicators. "I recognized that people like change when they see change as an opportunity for growth and a vital part of staying current and competitive. What people resist is the idea of *being changed*. Recognizing this, I taught all my employees a six-step communication process that allowed them to control outcomes. This process—which I called 'The Asking Formula' (and is now outlined in a book of the same name)—teaches people how to more effectively ask for what they want, drive their agendas, and maximize the positive outcomes in their lives. I made a special effort to teach my leaders The Asking Formula. When your team knows what you want, and is given the support and information necessary to deliver it, your entire organization moves through the change curve more rapidly and with more cohesion."

What also helped was how they created collaboration within the organization. "We broke down silos by linking everyone's goals to customer goals. For example, technology people typically reports on their technology agenda, and HR has HR goals to meet. Yet everyone was focused in some way on making the customer profitable and successful. This united focus made sure that if a technology person and HR person needed to collaborate, it wouldn't be a battle about whose priorities to focus on—they would both be focusing on customer priorities."

This united focus, on top of the business acumen, a trusting culture, and effective communication strategies, enabled Baker's business to keep both employees and customers satisfied, even during a difficult time.

Chapter 5
Energizing the Team

Lawrence was teaching a customer service class once a number of years ago in downtown Manhattan. One of the participants, Frank, a manager from Staten Island who spoke with a Soprano accent and just happened to own a pizzeria on the side (we're just saying…), raised his hand. He said, "People are like batteries. Many of our employees come to work drained from their personal responsibilities: money issues, problems with older parents, children, and then the commute. And we expect them to be energized on the job. Our job as managers, really, is to charge them up. To get them energized! If we don't do it, who will?"

Frank's comment captures the essence of this chapter. What can you do as a leader to get and keep employees energized? This chapter has three sections, each outlining practical strategies to help you keep your team energized:

- Lead with confidence.
- Design a winning team.
- Implement team energizer strategies.

Lead With Confidence

Mitch Pisik is a rapid retooler by profession. "I have made my living over the past 10 years by being hired by private equity firms to revamp their portfolios of companies." Pisik was hired a few years ago as the CEO of Breckwell Products, a manufacturer of pellet- and wood-burning stoves. It was a 30-year-old company bought by private equity two years earlier—specifically to turn around the company. One of the issues they had was old products. Nothing new had been developed in more than five years. The employees, to say the least, were not so motivated.

Pisik examined the financials, met with employees both in groups and one-on-one, talked to vendors, and held customer meetings. With everyone he talked to, he discussed the state of the industry, Breckwell's strengths and weaknesses, and those of the competition. He then talked about where they were headed financially if the business didn't change. His transparency and business-focused thinking built common understanding, a sense of community, and a sense of urgency in creating new products. Pisik realized that if they could develop a new, award-winning product, the success would reenergize the employees, attract new customers, and give sales a boost—in short, set the company on the road to recovery.

All new products in the industry are launched at an annual trade show. New products usually took a year from inception to selling. But they only had five months until the show. The obstacle seemed insurmountable. Pisik says, "I brought everyone together. There were about 100 people in the company. I knew some people would greet the challenge, but I also thought some might be skeptical. They hadn't had a new product in five years. It was difficult to imagine creating one in five months." Pisik explained the goal and the consequences of not meeting it to his employees. "You could feel the doubt in the room. So I told them, 'I believe we can do this. I will meet with each of you to go through the planning, timelines, what is expected of everyone, what tools you need to make this a success.'" He ended on a personal note. "'I moved my whole family from New York to Texas to help this company. I would not have done it if I didn't have faith in you. I have accomplished goals like this in other companies in other industries. And we are going to do it here!'

"They were never challenged like this before. But I believed they were smart enough and capable enough to do it. They just needed someone who believed in them and the company. I was that person."

This new product wasn't just the engineers' project or Pisik's project. It was everyone's project. He pulled in vendors for ideas on materials and manufacturing. Sales staff brought in customers to find out what features and benefits they wanted in products that were not yet available in the market. Every employee, aware of his or her role, rallied behind the project.

Pisik also had to make sure they had the tools they needed to succeed. There wasn't a big budget to play with so he had to allocate their resources wisely. He decided to invest in new technology that would track the air flow of stoves. This technology helped engineers come up with a new product that wouldn't wreck their budget. The fact that the CEO was investing in them also gave the engineers confidence and a fresh surge of determination.

An engineer came through with a design for the first prototype. Operations came up with manufacturing approaches, and vendors came up with new ideas for it. "In this industry all the stoves are big black ugly square boxes. So we designed one that had a tall cylinder shape, with a rounded door, not square. Then we built it." The stove was ready two hours before the show. The final, last-minute innovation was to paint it red. There were no red stoves on the market. The bright new color would get people in the booth at the show.

The result? Breckwell won the award for best-in-show for new stoves. Mitch brought back the plaque and hung it outside the office of the engineer who had designed the stove. The victory was written up in all the trade magazines and the new stove accounted for 25 percent of sales in the next year (a huge chunk considering the company had 29 other products on the market). The team was so pumped up that they started challenging themselves to create new products and improve existing processes. Their energy and passion simply needed to be uncovered by a leader who had confidence in them.

RR Recommendation

Paul Beauchamp, Partner at Deloitte & Touche LLP, says, "Confidence and humility are both critical. You need humility to ask questions and to listen, and you need confidence to take risks when implementing what you have learned. I am always looking for mentors and I might have many of them at any given time. I am also cognizant that I am serving my staff in this role and that it is a large responsibility. How I react to conflict, how I solve problems, and how I manage my time will be observed and possibly emulated."

We also know of a talented manager in China, Harrison Park, who led his team through extremely adverse circumstances to fulfill their obligation to a valued customer. Park knew that when you spot resistance, you can choose to give up or you can choose to rise to the occasion. He chose to rise to the occasion.

It was the end of January and many of the major commercial centers of China were virtually shut down by a snowstorm. The army had to be called in to shovel the main roads. On top of that, it was the Chinese New Year. Everyone was heading home for their annual family visit.

This facility in China had been trying for two years to close a deal with a key customer, and they had finally succeeded. But now they needed to deliver the product in one week, despite the storm, road closures, and the national holiday. How could they do it?

Park made it happen. He told us, "I said to myself, 'What do we have to lose by trying?' If we make it, the customer will be very pleased and see how committed we are to them. If we don't make it, the customer will understand what we were up against. So I asked my manager if I could try. He said yes and so I began."

He brought his team together. The first thing he did was ask them if they would try to produce the order for the customer. They told him it was impossible, for the reasons listed above. But Park was not deterred. He stressed again how important this customer was. He told them that if they could do it, they would win over this key customer, and it would bring them a lot of business in the future. He also promised to give them time off after the delivery was completed.

So the team agreed to try. First, they contacted the government to call in a favor so they could have some roads shoveled. Next, they found a trucker to transport the material. They paid extra because of the snow and the Chinese New Year. And finally, the managers ran the facility with a skeleton crew.

In the end, the materials made it to the customer as promised. They were so impressed that they committed to an even larger order for the next month. The extra business was won due to leadership, teamwork, and not taking "no" for an answer.

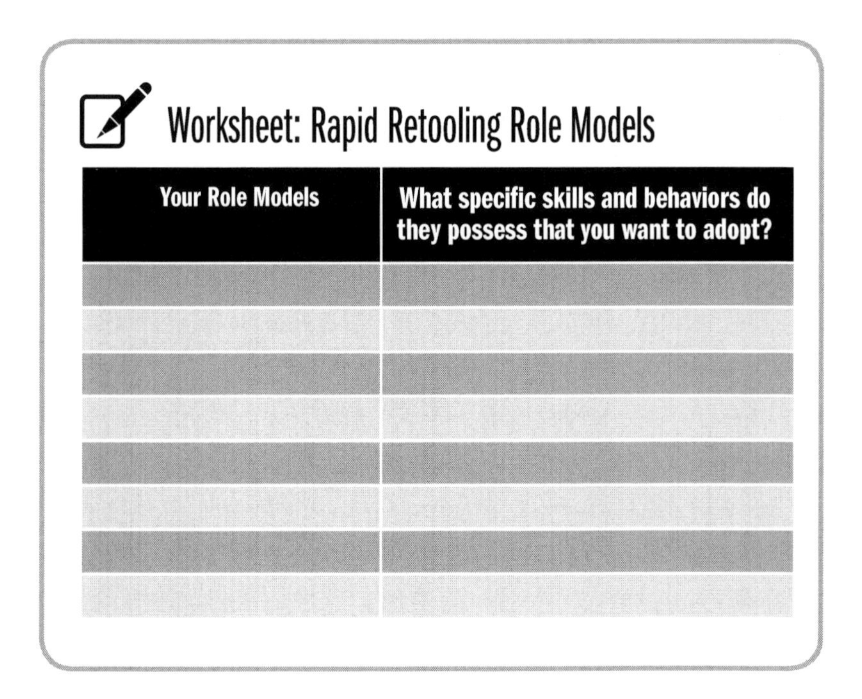

Worksheet: Rapid Retooling Role Models

Your Role Models	What specific skills and behaviors do they possess that you want to adopt?

Design a Winning Team

Rapid retooling does not happen without the cooperation of your team. But what about putting change completely in their hands? Do you recall the Orange Regional Medical Center, which we discussed in an earlier chapter? The organization was going through large-scale change, including combining two hospital sites into one and implementing an electronic health record. To help make this big change work, they had the employees design the transition. Betsy Kennally, Director of Organizational Development, told us, "We chose a guided change approach, one that would tap into all employees. We had employees from each hospital work in teams with their counterparts to design the transition in their own units. We chose this method because we wanted to minimize declines in productivity or performance, while enhancing creativity and buy-in. Our guided approach helped us maintain steady people metrics (which we obtained through employee surveys), and I think that was because it enabled each team to move beyond thinking about what was necessary in this process to thinking about what was possible."

What Kind of Team Are You?

Dr. Urs Karkoschka is the Head of HR AMAC at Novartis Pharma AG. Karkoschka's responsibilities cover a huge territory, including all of Africa, Australia, New Zealand, all Southeast Asian countries, and the Middle East. Quick adjustments to satisfy new customers and respond to changing regulatory environments are important in defending or establishing industry leadership in this territory.

When asked how he achieves success in his role, Karkoschka did not hesitate a moment: "My number one reason for my success is a strong team!" He emphasized that he could not do his work without good chemistry between all his team members. "At the beginning, teamwork was poor. There was no alignment of values and goals, no clear definition of roles and responsibilities, and even though we had high personal trust, it wasn't enough. This led to a situation where I could not focus on important strategic topics. I had to get involved in a lot of operational details. It made me unhappy, and more importantly it made my boss unhappy. This persisted until we decided to go through a team-building program.

"We learned that it's not the team with the best most talented individuals that wins, but the team with the highest level of trust and mutual respect. Each of my team members had to better understand his or her role. Furthermore we all wanted to be aware of each team member's strengths and weaknesses. Collective self-awareness and trust are key, particularly in situations when you have to make quick decisions!"

The importance of trust in creating a team that can collectively make quick decisions is also apparent to the U.S. military. It is dramatically documented in the account of the Navy SEAL raid on Osama bin Laden in Abbottabad, Pakistan. Mark Owen, the now-retired Navy SEAL whose team conducted the raid, has related SEAL teamwork to a game of pickup basketball. In an interview with CBS News' *60 Minutes* Owen said, "We all know how to shoot. We all know how to move efficiently and tactically. And we can communicate clearly. So when something goes sideways, we're able to play pickup basketball and just kind of read off each other."

When we work with teams challenged by rapid change, we also employ a sports metaphor. We ask, "What kind of team are you? Golf team? Orchestra? Baseball? Dance? Soccer?" And more importantly, "What kind of team do you need to be?" We use the chart on the opposite page to help the team make more conscious choices about how they collaborate, communicate, problem solve, and make decisions. Any adjectives can be written in the cells; here are some examples to get your team started. It doesn't matter which team you choose to be. If your team is facing the need to act quickly and adapt to new situations, you just need to be clear and agree on which one you want to be.

	Golf	Orchestra	Baseball	Soccer
Collaboration	Little	Led	Role-based	Spontaneous
Communication	Before/After	Watch/Listen	Watch/Listen	Spontaneous
Problem Solving and Decision Making	With coach	Before	Spontaneous	Spontaneous
Leadership	Low	Strong	Coaching	Shared

Winning teams are often formed rapidly at consulting companies, and often with stunning results. It is their daily business to quickly gather expert knowledge about a given topic. Many times they find themselves confronted with unprecedented challenges. How do they tackle these challenges and deliver solutions for their clients?

More advice from John Morgan: "We have the best repositories of data, latest research, best practices, and so forth. However, some of the best information lives undocumented in the minds of our consultants. We have very frequent opportunities to demonstrate this *esprit de corps*, or team spirit. There is heavy, heavy encouragement to reach out if you are having an issue. And if you do reach out, people respond. People you'd never met and you may never meet. They may be extremely busy executives, but our culture is such that if somebody is asking you for help or guidance, you'll figure out how to accommodate them. I've never had anybody say no.

"For example, I had a call this morning from Europe, from a guy I hadn't met before. He asked, 'Can I meet with you because I understand you know a lot about networks?' I asked him to send me a couple of questions so I could prepare. A few minutes later we spoke. This kind of collaboration energizes you because it shows you that you are never alone!"

"What Would You Do If You Owned the Company?"

Independence and entrepreneurialism are significant motivators and contributors to rapid retooling. Employees act faster when they are equipped with enough business acumen and independence to assess situations, interpret them, and immediately take action themselves, or approach their supervisor or other people in the company to do so.

Antoine was coaching a manager around this issue recently. He was kind of passive, waiting for instructions and not initiating actions. This had been a challenge since he began in his role. His department was a few months from a major deadline, but it was unclear if they would make it. So Antoine asked him, "What would you do if you owned the company?"

This simple question forced him, and will force you, to think like an entrepreneur. When companies are faced with urgent deadlines and restricted resources, they need employees to think like this. In fact, in many of our team retreats, we end the sessions with the question, "What can *you* do to help the team progress?" We ask this question because we found early on in our consulting that when we asked, "What has to be done to move the team forward?" most employees would give ideas on what management or other people had to do. This expectation that someone else should change or lead the change is a recipe for really slow retooling, not rapid retooling.

Why are we writing about entrepreneurialism here and not in the chapter on business acumen? We want to emphasize the power that entrepreneurial freedom has to motivate people and how it can increase solution options by putting ownership on many more shoulders. Cultivating a spirit of entrepreneurialism in employees will use their potential to the fullest.

Bringing the Olympic Spirit to Your Workplace

Since 1976, McDonald's has been an official restaurant partner of the Olympic Games. At the 2012 London games, there was a lot of rapid retooling going on behind the scenes at McDonald's. Not only would they have to choose 2,500 of their best employees to work the four McDonald's at the Olympic Park, they would assist in training 70,000 volunteers at the Olympic Park. For the first time in Olympic history, McDonald's in the U.K. became the official partner for what is called the Games Maker Program. To select, hire, train and support those 70,000 people in a very short time frame was a tremendous challenge. McDonald was chosen to be the Games Maker training partner because of their world-class training expertise within the hospitality industry. The program prepared the volunteers from all walks of life to put their best foot forward throughout the Olympic venues.

We spoke to Jez Langhorn, VP of People at McDonald's in the U.K., to hear him explain how McDonald's went about choosing employees to work at the Olympics. "We started an Olympic Champion Crew Member of the Month program. We have 1,200 restaurants in the U.K. (about two-thirds of which are owned and operated by local businessmen and women). Each store, over the course of 12 months, designated an Olympic Champion Crew Member of the Month. At the end of the year-long period, we brought together every store's 12 Champion crew members for regional team competitions. The best of the best competed to show off their skills and were judged by our franchisees, corporate staff, and our training teams. We then selected 2,500 crew members from that group to work in our Olympic restaurants."

Employees had the honor of serving Olympians like Usain Bolt as he bought his chicken wrap before his 100-meter run. Their travel, food, and lodging expenses were taken care of, and they each received a free ticket to an Olympic event. Employees were also asked to download a mobile app designed specifically to help them schedule their shifts.

Langhorn explained other benefits of the competition: "The opportunity to work at the Olympics spurred employees to high levels of performance. Crew members competed with each other to be the best cashier or the best on the grill line. We've also found that turnover rates for the chosen Olympic champion crew were one-quarter of our average company turnover, which is already incredibly low. So clearly, this competition was a really good way of engaging our staff and keeping them motivated and performing at their best."

Elizabeth Greene, Director of Organizational Learning at Make-A-Wish International, also used fun and games to achieve operational excellence in the workplace. For example, they had "Office Olympics" during all two weeks of the Olympics, always at lunchtime. The CEO was involved as well as the other senior leaders, and they held medal ceremonies after each competition. Some of the competitions were focused on teambuilding, with chair races, mini-bowling, and jump rope. Greene said, "Invariably, when people got back to work, they had more energy and sharper focus."

Strategies to Energize Your Team

When change is looming on the horizon, getting your team started on the right foot is half the battle. Lawrence sat in on a change launch meeting recently and was blown away. The leader did everything we would ever suggest to make the launch a success. Here are the 12 things he said that made the meeting as close to perfect as possible.

12 Phrases for Rapid Retooling Meetings

1. Set meeting expectations. "Your head will probably be spinning when we are done. That is okay." It's funny, but when people know they will be overwhelmed, they won't crumple under the stress of feeling that way.

2. Set positive expectations for change success. "You will be confident and excited [by the time we are ready to implement]." Rarely have we heard a leader set a positive expectation for how employees will feel at the end of a change implementation. We found it refreshing and uplifting. Is it a bit "Pollyanna"? It can be. But in this case it came across as authentic and was well received.

3. Extend support. "We are here for you," to answer questions, coach you, help you, and so forth. The change launch leader said this multiple times throughout the hour-long meeting. The extra acknowledgement was reassuring.

4. Get peer testimony of past success. "Who has been through this process before? These are our role models. They are proof that you will all be okay when we are done." Our global research results correspond with this statement. People trust non-leaders more than formal leaders. It is a smart move to identify these non-leaders as helpful resources for employees experiencing change for the first time.

5. It is about us, not you. "We are all going through this." It was helpful to point out that employees shouldn't feel alone or the target of the change.

6. Give a brief but clear timeline. The leader had one double-sided page as a handout. It clearly highlighted key phases and steps in the change initiative for the next eight to 16 months. This showed his team that the change was manageable. He then discussed the handout with the team.

7. We are role models. The change leader said, "We expect you to be role models for people going through the change. They will take seriously what we take seriously." During rapid change, leaders are under a magnifying glass: every statement, action (or inaction), and even body language are closely observed and interpreted by your people. It is therefore critical to pay extra attention to what you are doing and not doing.

8. Review key learning activities. He reviewed the learning plan and timing. This gave everyone a good idea of the amount of work required and the sense that they would be well-prepared for their new responsibilities.

9. Acknowledge the workload. "I know everyone has a lot going on. We will work with you to make this work, and you will work with us." He acknowledged the amount of work involved and that the leadership would help. And that, despite the workload, he expected everyone to do their part.

10. Explain monitoring. There was a system in place to track progress of the plan. This was explained to let everyone know that management was on top of the change.

11. Be firm. "Are we serious about the expectations we have for each employee? Yes. There are consequences for failing to meet expectations." Some people will only do what is required if they know there are consequences, good or bad. Our 2012 global research showed that only 43 percent of organizations recognize employees who contribute positively to change initiatives, and only 34 percent dole out consequences when employees don't change as required.

12. End with positivity. His conclusion to the meeting was positive and inspiring. "You will all be prepared. You are all talented and capable. We say that positivity is contagious, as much as negativity is. So why not be positive?"

We know you veteran change leaders are saying, "These phrases alone do not make the implementation a success." And you are right! The proof is always in the follow-through. But that is not an excuse to give a weak launch. Taking these suggestions will help you start on the right foot. They address employee emotions, and focus on the actions that are critical for change success. They will ultimately help to reduce resistance and create positive momentum, which is the most you can ask for.

Interpreting Employee Complaints About Change

As you confidently lead your team, you will hear people complaining about how they like the old way better. When you do, give yourself a pat on the back. This means they have accepted that the change is happening, moved past their initial fears, and are struggling with how to make the change work for them.

A mistake leaders make is that when they hear complaining, they take it as a sign that people are resisting the change. It's actually quite the opposite. At the beginning of any change, when people are struggling with accepting it, complaining is normal and healthy. Everyone will have challenges with making the change work. As a leader, you want to know what those challenges are so you can help your employees succeed. Once progress is being made, if the complaining persists, then it is a sign that employees are resisting the change. This kind of behavior will have detrimental effects on performance. Here's how to differentiate between a normal struggle to adapt to change and flat-out resistance to change.

Adapting to Change	Resisting Change
Expressing discontent or difficulty...	
While working on making progress	With no intent of taking action or showing desire for progress
Yet willing to accept their role in improvement	And blaming others for the problem
But after expressing the issue, work with leader to work through the problem	And lacking constructiveness, helpfulness, optimism, or cooperativeness

We once conducted a change management workshop for a company in Europe where this issue of complaints came up. We were leading a cross-functional discussion about actions needed to support the change's success. The head of operations was clearly resisting suggestions made by the head of IT. We knew from previous meetings and conversations that both leaders were on board with the changes and willing to support the process. However, each time the IT person proposed a solution, the operations head would jump in and say, "Yes, I know that is a problem, but…" Then she would give all the reasons why the solution wouldn't work. We had to interrupt the discussion and say to the operations head, "The IT head is giving you ideas for improvement. Instead of interpreting the ideas as complaints, and dismissing them right off the bat, consider them. Otherwise, the suggestions will stop and so will the improvements and the success of the change."

This is a common challenge of leaders, especially technical leaders. They ascend the ranks by being smarter and by being right more often than others. Often, it is hard for them to listen to others' suggestions for improvements. Instead of hearing the idea, they hear a complaint, the message that "What you are doing now or have done in the past is wrong." This misinterpretation will slow down change progress, if not grind it to a screeching halt.

RR Recommendation

- Spend at least twice as long listening as speaking.
- Respond with conversation expanders, such as "Tell me what you mean by that."
- Try to repeat back the main feelings and thoughts expressed before responding.
- At team meetings, say, "Let's hear other people's points of view on this."

Eight Team Accelerators

Another major challenge in energizing employees is creating a sense of "we"—a sense of ownership. Many companies are spread across the world, under pressure to cut costs and increase revenue, and often must operate as siloed divisions. This kind of environment presents the challenge of unifying the organization. Leaders must ask themselves, "How do we create the feeling that we are all in this together?"

Here are eight practical strategies from organizational leaders to improve teamwork during rapid retooling:

1. Bring teams together to facilitate knowledge sharing. Lawrence was chatting with Mehul Mehta, a human resources lead at Xcelris Labs in India, when Mehta told him about a program he started in his biotech firm to address the issue of siloes and disengagement. It is called "Me to We." In Mehta's organization, they have monthly sessions for employees to come forward and share what they learned from their co-workers and give appreciation. Why? The teams are highly interdependent. They are working at a fast pace. Taking people out of their individual teams, and bringing them together to focus on knowledge sharing, creates an increased awareness of how each team affects the others. They are gaining a larger sense of "we," beyond their jobs and their own teams, resulting in more frequent and more efficient cross-functional collaboration. See chapter 4 for ideas on breaking down silos.

2. Create dialogue sessions to discuss business issues and challenges. Employees will feel a part of the "we" if you include them in the business. Mike Nestor, Head of Change at Bayer, uses this approach to create team spirit. "When we are rolling out changes in teams or divisions, we hold dialogue sessions where the strategy is discussed in detail, with data showing why this strategy was chosen. External market conditions, actions from competitors, internal pressures, and shareholder expectations are all discussed," says Nestor. "Significant time is devoted to dialogue where employees and leaders share perspectives and in some cases personal feelings (passions, fears, concerns, opportunities)." This involvement and education leaves employees feeling part of the team, because they are!

3. Let team members select those who join the team. Merrimack Pharmaceuticals in Cambridge, MA, designed their organization around teams. They are trying to innovate and commercialize new medicines. The faster the better is always the case for this kind of startup. The sooner high-quality products can get to marketplace, the better. To ensure the team will be optimal, they include team members in the hiring of new team members.

Andy Porter, VP of Human Resources, said, "We have seen excellent results using the power of small teams focused on a specific goal. To this end, we initiated a unique selection process where team members interview and select their new teammates. This creates a true commitment to each other."

4. Talk in terms of "we," "us," and "team." As a team leader, your words make a huge difference. How you talk about the team impacts the team. Jerry Ganguzza, Service Manager of Skyline Exhibits of Los Angeles, knew the power of using language that motivates and unifies the team. When he came on board, he noticed a disconnect between sales and service. There was a lack of trust and no camaraderie. Ganguzza settled on a solution that was just as simple as it was speedy: He began calling both groups "Team L.A." "Immediately, there was a sense of shared responsibility for our sales and service functions," he said.

5. Hold face-to-face meetings. Virtual communication only goes so far! Face-to-face interactions lend more depth and richness to team relationships. There are more opportunities for personal bonds to form, which often leads to more loyalty, willingness to accommodate each other's ideas and concerns, and higher productivity levels back at the office.

6. Push information out. This is what Allen Dye, VP of Sales at Corporate Floors, does. "With a remote sales team, I'm much more conscious of communicating what's going on within our organization, and sharing wins, ideas, and best practices," says Dye. "It sounds simple, and it is. Sometimes it's via email and sometimes it's through a personal phone call. It keeps people feeling in the loop."

7. Involve the team in setting organizational direction. Most of us know that people are more committed to solutions they develop. This is particularly true when you are a new leader and team members are hundreds of miles apart. Marc Chasin, MD, SVP, and Chief Medical Information Officer at St. Luke's Health System, knew this as well. When he started in his new role a few months ago, he had a new team, spread across the state of Idaho. How was he going to get them to feel and act like a team? His main objective was rolling out a new electronic health record through their health system. This was a major change for the doctors, nurses, and all the staff. What he did and continues to do is solicit and incorporate the team's opinions and suggestions, and use them to form the departmental vision and mission. "This way, it is our project, not my project."

8. Rotate responsibility across the team. While working with an executive team to improve their teamwork during rapid change, we realized one of their problems was their weekly meeting. The leader felt that the team was not taking initiative. The team felt like the leader was overbearing. So our simple approach was to help them share responsibility, beginning with the weekly meeting. Each of the six team members took a turn at defining the issues that need to be addressed at the meetings. They also rotate minute-taking. This simple adjustment has dramatically improved the meeting's efficiency. It is no longer thought of as "his meeting" but has morphed into "our meeting."

Being part of a team is something that people can sense and feel. You can't demand it or enforce it. It has to happen organically and come from the team members themselves. Using these eight strategies will help create an environment where people feel part of something larger than themselves and therefore more committed to your organization's goals and overall vision.

Six Individual Accelerators

Let's end the "team chapter" by getting back to the individual team member. One of the main reasons change fails is lack of individual buy-in. So what can you do to get real buy-in for rapid retooling and organizational changes? We asked seasoned internal change leaders for their input and this is what they told us.

1. Explain options and consequences. The biggest mistake leaders make is that they don't explain employees' options and their consequences during times of change, says Mike Nestor, Head of Change at Bayer. "So what I have started doing with managers is to have them say to their employees, 'Here are your choices and here are the consequences to the organization, your team, and yourself.' Knowing the impact of their choices increases buy-in. Employees know what will happen depending on what they choose to do."

2. Do the right thing. Erik Gillet, Global Head of Operational Excellence & Quality in the accounting division of Credit Suisse, focuses on helping employees do the right thing, based on their job role. He says, "In my experience, we have driven change too much by dangling carrots. There is at least one more approach that perhaps can be labeled 'role identification.' I find that employees often do something simply because it is the right thing to do. As leaders, finding or triggering that feeling creates a powerful attitude towards accepting change."

3. Analyze stakeholders. IT-based change is a challenge for many reasons. A top one is lack of the right kind of stakeholder commitment, says Amy Solomon, IT Training Manager at Tenneco. She explained that for every change implementation, she does a very specific buy-in analysis. First, they examine the key stakeholders and determine if they are actively resisting, passively accepting, contributing to the change happen, or leading the change. This provides the data for a buy-in plan, to ensure the right people are bought in at the right level.

4. Wish away problems. Abha Mehta, Director of Business Operations at Nokia Mobile Payment Services, says that the simplest way to generate buy-in is to create a shared vision of what the desired destination will look like. "It begins by identifying pain points of today and showing how the future will improve these pain points or better...

remove them completely. This is a sure-shot way of gaining buy-in as everyone wants to 'wish away' some of their current problems!"

5. Listen up. Doug Bush, conflict resolution and performance management expert at an organization in NYC, says to keep it simple. "Let employees know that they are valued members of the team by listening to and addressing their concerns, needs, and interests. Then, ask for their commitment to the hard work ahead, each step of the way. This works much better than trying to sell them on your ideas."

6. Enable employee-driven change. In their stores, Staples has an "easy button" for focusing on employee ideas. Ray Stevens, previous Director of Staples' SellingXchange, explained their approach: "We use an online method of identifying change, which creates a high level of buy-in. We have a social media forum where employees can make suggestions on things to change and improve. The ideas with the most 'likes' get presented to the leadership. Then, the leadership chooses if they want to implement ideas from this list. This doesn't guarantee that the ideas will be picked, but it does create a high level of buy-in, since the ideas were generated and 'approved' first by employees."

Worksheet: How's My Leadership?

Team Energizer Strategies	How am I doing?
When leading change launch meetings, I will... 1. Set expectations for the meeting. 2. Set positive expectations for change success. 3. Extend support to my team. 4. Use peer testimony of past success. 5. Focus on "us," not "me." 6. Create a clear, brief timeline to complete tasks and projects. 7. Be a role model. 8. Review key learning opportunities. 9. Acknowledge the workload. 10. Explain how I will be monitoring change progress. 11. Be firm. 12. End with positivity.	
Team Accelerators 1. Bring teams together to facilitate knowledge sharing. 2. Create dialogue sessions to discuss business issues and challenges. 3. Let team members select those who join the team. 4. Talk in terms of "we," "us," and "team." 5. Hold face-to-face meetings. 6. Push information out. 7. Involve the team in setting organizational direction. 8. Rotate responsibility across the team.	
Individual Accelerators 1. Explain options and consequences. 2. Do the right thing. 3. Analyze stakeholders. 4. Wish away problems. 5. Listen up. 6. Enable employee-driven change.	

Chapter 6
Making It Personal

In a business world where companies and people are rapidly retooling, you need to have energy, enthusiasm, and excitement to succeed. But this is not enough. You have to find ways to stay energized as you face the constant challenges of rapid change. This is especially true if you are in a leadership position, as your team will feed on your energy and enthusiasm (or lack thereof).

How you choose to fuel your energy and passion is very personal. What works for one person or company may be a disaster for another. Given the complexity of people's personalities, life and career goals, and organizational situations, this chapter discusses general approaches you can take to maintain positive energy, instead of providing specific strategies which may or may not work for you. Here are four questions to consider that will help shape your approach to remaining energized at work.

- How do you integrate your work and your personal life?
- Do you match talent with job requirements and culture?
- How much control do you give employees regarding how and when they work?
- What kind of personal attributes are needed to thrive in a rapidly changing environment?

Integrating Work and Personal Life

Faber-Castell USA conducted a survey of its employees as preparation for designing a new EAP (Employee Assistance Program). In the survey, the area that employees indicated they would most like assistance in was the area of work-life balance. Jamie Gallagher, CEO of Faber-Castell USA, was not surprised. "As business becomes more challenging we are asking more of our employees. More complex problems and assignments also lead to an increased amount of time they are spending at work and thinking of work while away from work."

Is Work-Life Balance Possible?

A director of training we spoke to recently summed up what a lot of people say to us: "There is no work-life balance because I'm never shut off from work. Emails, text messages, phone calls can always reach me. Just managing my email is a full-time job in itself. I'm just trying to keep my emails under 400 in any given day. My vice president sends me emails at 11 o'clock at night. Obviously I have the choice of responding or not responding. But my experience is that if I don't respond immediately, then it's piled up in the morning and I've got more to take care of first thing in the morning."

People talk about work-life balance because they feel they have too much work, not enough play. Too much time in the office, not enough time at home. But some executives believe that it is about work-life integration, not balance. What is balance, anyway? Eight hours at work, eight hours at home, and eight hours sleeping? Does anyone live like this?

Vern Dosch, CEO, National Information Solutions Cooperative (NISC) used one of his recent internal blogs to reflect on work-life integration in his organization.

It was 1988, and I was sitting in a night class on Human Resources when I first heard the phrase work-life balance. The professor was passionate about helping us understand the importance of balancing the commitment we make to our employer and our dedication to our personal lives. I found the discussion fascinating, but very different from my personal understanding of work. Let me explain. As I was getting ready for my first day on the job at Capital Electric in 1975, my father called and gave me the following instructions: "A job is a privilege, keep your head down, work as many hours as required, never complain, don't ask dumb questions, and don't even think about taking a vacation until you have been on the job for at least two years."

Throughout my career in the '70s and '80s my father's instructions always resonated with me. Number of hours worked was like a red badge of courage, the more the better. Somehow, in our minds, the number of hours you worked equated to your dedication and value to the organization. In the '90s we began our connection addiction. The hours away from the office were invaded by the ubiquitous ability to receive and send email or connect to the office network. Now, the detached solitude of travel meant that your new office was the vehicle or the airport concourse. My work life, which was already out of balance, was now on full tilt.

Recently I read the book Off Balance *by Mathew Kelly and found it completely contradictory to my former impression of work-life balance. Kelly shows that the reality of the work-life balance that's been discussed for the past 20 years has been nothing but a fallacy. The basic premise of this discussion is work is bad, your life is good and you must not have too much bad in your life. And by the way, you must also separate your work life from your private life.*

Does work have to be bad and dreaded, something you must marginalize in order to have a good life? I'm of the opinion it is difficult if not impossible to separate work and your private life. If work is going badly, I promise you it will affect your personal life, and if your personal life is in the dumps, I guarantee it will affect your work life.

I ask you to consider a radical concept—work can and should be fun, invigorating, fulfilling, not a drag. And to a large degree, I think it is the employer's responsibility to create a work environment where an individual actually looks forward to Monday morning, where work is a challenge and a stretch, and individuals go home feeling spent and with the knowledge that they have added value to the organization. An individual's personal life affords them the time to separate from work and actually be focused and present for their family and friends rather than physically present and mentally back at the office. In addition, time away from work should provide the time and freedom to pursue personal interests and make a dent in "bucket lists" in a way that revitalizes and reenergizes. Sound radical? I don't think so.

I believe that work is very important. It's how we pay the bills, educate our kids, plan for the future and hopefully, enhance our personal time through vacations, hobbies, entertainment, and so forth. But more importantly, work provides an opportunity to grow, learn and feel a tremendous sense of satisfaction about the contribution we are making... yes, we all want to make a difference. I don't think it has to be either I love my work and hate my private life, or I hate my work and love my private life. Why can't it be both? Why can't we enjoy and be challenged by our work and relish our lives away from the office?

As an employer, I want you to know that NISC is committed to creating a work environment that is comfortable, productive and enjoyable, a work environment that you are proud of. We are beginning to understand that that environment is about doing meaningful work, providing opportunities to grow and learn, and having a coach that truly cares about you and your future as well as the success of the organization you serve. It is also about paying attention to details from very substantial considerations like compensation and benefits to what kind of coffee we make available and community engagement we facilitate for our employees.

And while I said I believe to a large degree it is an employer's responsibility, I believe a great work life requires the engagement of all individuals. Each individual needs to take initiative and an active role in defining their career and establishing the value they deliver each day. Creating a work-life balance is about an engaged employee who comes to work and leaves it all on the field, so to speak, then heads home where they can enjoy the fruits of their labors.

Thanks for listening!

Vern
CEO NISC
NISC Community blog, August 2012

One of our interviewees has a more pragmatic point of view: "The cost of a work-life imbalance is not borne by the company; it is borne by the employee. It doesn't show on our company's balance sheet. However, workforce demographic changes (baby boomers retiring in droves and younger employees entering the workforce with different values and expectations) leads to an increased need to reevaluate this issue."

Matching Talent With Job Requirements and Culture

Vala Ashfar, Chief Customer Officer at Enterasys, also believes in work-life integration. An executive leader in a fast-paced, growing business, he believes that the key to contentment is having expectations and values that are in sync with the needs of the job.

"I'm always connected when I'm awake. And as long as the work you're doing is meaningful to you, it doesn't seem like work. I can email at eight o' clock in the evening while my two-, six-, and nine-year-olds are climbing over my head. And I don't feel bad about it because if it's helping our company or an individual connected to the company, it just doesn't seem like work."

How does this work ethic go over with family? "Behind every good man there's an exceptional woman," he smartly replied. "My wife works hard at Harvard University in a demanding, critical function. So clearly we are both career-oriented. It's an alignment of values. Both of our parents worked really hard for really long. My parents worked until they were nearly 70, and we want to do our very best to achieve as much as we can as early as we can. It just takes an incredible amount of mutual understanding."

Michael, the head of Global HR in a 7,000-employee global manufacturing company, agrees with Ashfar. Being an ice-cream lover, he uses this analogy to describe work-life integration: "I think of it as two scoops of ice cream melting together. If you leave them, they melt and then they mix. So it's less and less a clear separation between business life and private life as it used to be 10, 20, or 30 years ago. Nowadays, from the moment you wake up you are connected by one or even several media. And not only during a normal working day, but also on weekends, holidays, vacations. It's interesting to see how people handle that differently. At the executive level you must stay connected in order for the company to run. You can maybe disconnect for a day or two. But that is the max. At lower levels disconnecting for longer periods of time is more possible."

But what about burnout? How do you prevent it? We know Michael's company is run very lean, and management works very hard and travels a lot. Michael told us, "I'm not aware of a single case of burnout at management level in our company, which is actually surprising. My opinion is that burnout occurs not because of too much work, but because of a mismatch between an employee's expectations and capabilities, and the expectations of the boss or company."

This opinion is consistent with our experience. We have run into many burnt-out employees because their priorities have changed. This means that their jobs don't work for them anymore.

Michael also has a very interesting point of view on employee engagement for a head of HR: No programs and no training. "You have to let people organize it the way it's best for them. But, of course, only within the boundaries that are good for the company. It's difficult to issue directives. I don't think you can do that. Over time, I believe people will come to understand whether they can match the expectations of the company they have joined. And sooner or later, only those who can match those expectations will be successful in the company. It becomes a natural selection process."

Ashfar also feels this way. "We've had executives that come here for job opportunities and during the interview they say, 'I don't really like to have a mobile phone because I like to shut down when I leave work.' But that doesn't work for our company. It's not the reality we live in."

Matching Employee Interests, Goals, and Skills to the Job

FedEx helps with work-life integration by matching employees' interests and skills to their jobs. Doing so increases satisfaction and morale and reduces stress. To help employees understand the realities of different jobs, they created the Center for Employee Self-Development. Bob Bennett, CLO and VP of HR, says, "The program encourages employees to think, 'What do I want to be when I grow up?' This resource lists all the jobs and functions that we have in the company, so an employee can look at everything and then say, 'Hey, I think I want to become an engineer.' He can click on that engineering button, and read about the roles and responsibilities and required competencies of an engineer. In some cases there are videos of what different jobs entail. Many times employees can click through to various resources for certain jobs, such as articles and training course descriptions. The Center for Employee Self-Development helps us create an environment in which employees are responsible for their own career development. But FedEx is trying to facilitate this as much as possible."

John Morgan, a telecommunication consultant, told us, "One of the biggest challenges in our business is that we hire the traditional type A personality—extremely smart, with a record of achievement and leadership. Those are the types of people who fit the mold in consulting. There is more and more demand for them. At the same time, the number one goal in life for these people is not necessarily to make it to the office and make a million dollars a year (anymore). We are seeing a rapid change with kids coming out of college today. They are more about life balance than hard work. What I hear is: 'I'm not necessarily interested in giving you 60 hours a week plus weekends; that's not my goal. I would much rather have a job that interests and challenges me, at some place where I can build my skills, but it's also a place where at five o'clock on Friday afternoon I can sign off and go do something else outside of work.'"

Morgan continued, "In this field, you'd either ride it up to the consultant ranks or you'd probably leave at some point because you didn't want to deal with the extensive travel and erratic hours this kind of career demands. At our company, since we've begun to employ younger generations who are more interested in maintaining a full life outside of work, we try to give employees more mobility between the various positions within the company. This allows employees to switch to jobs that fit changes in their lifestyles as they grow with us, so that we don't have high-level turnover. There has also been a push to source locally and to try to make better use of all the technology that we've got available to us, so that we put less demand on our employees to travel."

Recall the BMW plant in Spartanburg, SC that manufactures most of the X models in the world (the X3, X5 and X6)? We spoke of their innovation and collaboration challenge in the previous chapter. But they also had a labor challenge: It is becoming difficult to find qualified line workers who can keep up with changing technologies. The days of screwdrivers and power tools are gone. Yes, they still use those. But they also extensively use robotics and computers. Werner Eikenbusch, Manager of Apprenticeship and Associate Training at BMW's U.S. factory, says that there is a "short supply in the labor market of skilled trade, particularly something like maintenance in advanced manufacturing. This is now a very high-tech profession where you need to understand robots, POCs, PLCs, and so forth, but you also still need to be able to do the mechanical things. And, we use proprietary technology that you can't really pick up on the street if you are outside of the company."

To equip their line workers with the appropriate skills, BMW instituted an apprenticeship program. It is widely used in Europe, where really there is a choice between graduating from high school with no special skills and a four-year degree for learning a trade. In Europe, there is this whole level of skill trade that is really not very developed in the U.S., particularly in manufacturing. So they took what worked there and implemented it in South Carolina. The program is already a success: They graduated the first group of 14 students in the summer of 2012 and hired all of them as full-time associates. The program is currently expanding to its planned size of 70 apprentices.

Partnering with technical colleges in the community, they sponsored some of students working toward associate degrees. The students agree to on-the-job training (paid) of about 20 hours per week. They get to apply theories they learn in the classroom with on-the-job training at BMW. At the end of the program, they could be offered a job, continue on to a four-year degree, or find employment with another company. Hopefully, they would decide to work at BMW. The apprenticeship program fills the need for changing workplace skills and helps BMW grow and continue to succeed in a fast-paced economy.

Employee Control of How and When They Work

We had the pleasure of working with David Kappos and his executives to support their organizational change. Kappos is Under Secretary of Commerce for Intellectual Property and Director of the U.S. Patent and Trademark Office. He has a selfless approach that involves empowering his employees: "Regardless of who is in charge here, whether it is me or someone else, they can take what they are learning, and the changes we implemented together, and it will help them and the organization succeed in the future. As a political appointee, I may eventually move on. But they will still be here to run this organization."

Kappos is a role model for us for two reasons. Number one, he is committed to his team and the long-term success of the organization. Secondly, his goal is not to make himself irreplaceable. Instead, he is working so that he can be easily replaced. This takes guts and self-confidence. He is allowing his employees to take ownership of the organization, giving them the tools and power and support they need so they can carry on despite changes in leadership.

RR Recommendation

The new owner and CEO of a European high-tech company was in desperate need of a quick orientation to the company and its industry. "When I bought this company I had no clue about it or the market in which we operate. I had no other option but to ask my people: '*What would you do?*' I was astonished by the wealth of information and advice they gave me. And most surprisingly was that many people told me that they had never been asked the questions I was asking. They were untapped resources of information and insight."

Instead of struggling alone, he asked for help from his employees. Who are the people in your surroundings whom you have never asked for help? Discover their untapped potential and knowledge! We guarantee that they will contribute to your personal rapid retooling.

There is a growing amount of literature that concludes that working less means working more efficiently. One example is an article that was published in the *New York Times* in August 2012, titled, "Be More Productive. Take Time Off," in which the writer and entrepreneur Jason Fried describes how his software company 37Signals improved employee productivity by reducing work hours. Their offices are in Chicago, where the winters are hard and long. So from May to October, Mr. Fried instituted a four-day work week of 32 hours per week. He believes this shortened week helps employees focus on top priorities.

We also know of a high-tech start-up, located in Princeton, NJ, where the owner walks around the office and kicks employees out at 5:30. He believes that everyone needs time away from work to recharge their batteries.

20 Percent Time

Google coined the idea "20 percent time." Software developers can spend one day a week working on projects that aren't necessarily in their job descriptions. They can develop something new or fix something they know is broken. This not only generates new services for Google such as Gmail, it also helps address work-life integration. Software developers are creative and love to have freedom in their jobs. By allowing their software developers to tinker with projects close to their hearts and outside of their routine tasks, Google channels their creativity into new business opportunities, while at the same time maximizing their job satisfaction.

There is a New York City agency that has a similar challenge. They hire very smart, highly educated professionals who are specialists in their field. To attract them, and keep them motivated, one of the top leaders at the agency told us, "We have an informal approach to talent retention, of which all employees are aware: If employees are interested in working on something that's tangential, it can't be totally irrelevant. They can't just stand up and say they want to start a modern art collection. But if they are interested in one of the problems, opportunities, or challenges we face and they want to spend some time exploring new and innovative ways to approach them, we will give them as much time and resources as possible so that they can deliver a worthwhile result. That being said, if they demonstrate poor performance and lack of motivation, we take away the opportunity to explore issues that are of interest to them."

RR Recommendation

Here's a new interpretation of the 20 percent rule: You have envisioned the perfect solution to an organizational challenge or opportunity. But before marshaling the time, energy, and resources necessary to implement this solution, consider this: 80 percent of the ideal solution may be just good enough. To try to go for the additional 20 percent may be a drain of your resources. Setting these boundaries will not only preserve your employees' sanity, it will give them the time and energy to focus on solving 80 percent of other challenges. Recall our example from chapter one, in which John Balian shortened a three-year project to six months. The three-year timeline allowed for the "perfect" solution that would still have drained the company's resources down to nothing. John's solution addressed the most critical concerns, cutting out the fluff.

Stress Management

High-performing athletes schedule in recovery time. So why not high-performing leaders? Olympians don't work 12-hour days. They work hard for four to six hours, on average. Their downtime allows their bodies to recover from the stress and their energy levels to recharge. Recovery time for leaders can be scheduled too. Instead of time to repair physically, it is time to reflect, read, and explore ideas. This keeps them energized and innovative.

An executive team member at a global manufacturing company admits, "It's not always easy! The theory is easy, but putting it into practice is very challenging, especially when a company is going through challenging times or a lot of growth. You need to try to balance. The higher I am on the ladder the more difficult it has become. And I see this more and more with my colleagues as well. It is important to communicate that you don't want to only work. Once you start to 'out yourself' you'll discover that this is very much accepted. Nobody can work around the clock. Quality will go down, mistakes will happen, misunderstanding and frustration will be generated. It can be the beginning of a vicious cycle. Completely against the rapid retooling notion! Warning signs are people becoming edgy, tight, and tense. This behavior means they probably need time away from the office. Don't create a culture in which employees are afraid to speak openly about the importance of taking time off."

For some of us, it is hard to accept that we have to learn to go slower before we can go faster. Ancient Greeks and Romans knew that it takes a healthy body to have a healthy mind. Rapidity and alertness of mind requires a healthy person, or else rapidity and alertness can be quickly lost.

Teleworking

The Trademarks division of the U.S. Patent & Trademark Office runs their organization remotely.

Ninety percent of their examining attorneys telework full time. It is widely considered one of the leading government telework programs. Deborah Cohen, Commissioner for Trademarks, talked to us about how this affects work-life integration. "First off, we have such a large percentage of teleworkers that we were able to give up quite a large

RR Recommendation

The three major religions believe God created the world in six days, and on the seventh day he rested. Is there something we can learn from this? We think so. We take every Saturday as our day to rest: no email, no business meetings, no business phone calls, nothing. Try it for yourself. Decide what "rest" means for you. It's different things to different people. A big part of resting is to go offline. Try to create a "smartphone-free zone." Start with a few hours, always the same day and time a week (such as Friday evening after work until getting up the next morning). Once you are comfortable with a few hours you may want to extend it.

Clients of ours have experimented with email-free hours across their organizations, or with single days (such as Thursday and Friday) when they tell key contributors to focus their work on innovation and strategic activities and leave the more transactional obligations for other days. Take a few days to diligently monitor how much of your time goes into emails and other online media. Is there a way to create a non-interruption zone for yourself or your entire organization at work?

amount of office space when we set up our new offices in Crystal City (just outside Washington, D.C.) in 2004. We use state-of-the-art tools to keep our remote employees involved, and we have a very robust way of measuring our performance. We measure both the quality of the work and the quantity of the work, so the productivity of the employee is measured the same way whether they're working at the office or remotely. Telework gives you a better way to balance work and your personal life, so that you don't have to choose between having time with your family and being a hard-working, dedicated employee."

Like the Trademark division, the Patent side also has a telework program. In 2011, 2,600 patent examiners were participating in the program. In fact, their own audit found that the average participant in the program spends 66.3 more hours a year examining patents than does the average in-house examiner; this translates to about 3.5 more patent applications reviewed each year.

Telework is not without its disadvantages, however. One of the biggest complaints of managers and employees in virtual work situations is isolation. Managers at many organizations we work with complain that employees get out of the loop and seem disengaged. Employees themselves have the same complaint. At the Trademarks division, Deborah says, "We really try to keep employees engaged by promoting the collegiality of the organization. One of the programs we just started is ®Friend (like the ® for trademarks). We have a coordinator in each geographic area of the country that has teleworkers who organizes get-together events. So for example, if we have teleworkers in Seattle, the coordinator there will organize a lunch so that employees can meet and socialize with other local employees."

Personal Attributes for Rapid Retooling

Do you have what it takes? This is what leaders ask themselves, job applicants, and their team members when faced with the challenges of change. Having worked with and for many leaders of rapid change, we have found several personal attributes that you can hone to rapidly retool yourself and your organization.

Dynamic Leapfrogging

Louis Tafuto, the 2011 top U.S. Sprint Triathlete, is working toward being on the 2016 Olympic team. He is what we call a "dynamic leapfrogger." To compete at his level, one needs to leapfrog over unforeseen obstacles. For example, one day while riding his bike down a hill, Tafuto flew around a corner and hit a car head on—going 30mph. He went flying onto the road and was rushed to the hospital. They spent a few hours picking gravel out of his back, but he had no debilitating injuries from the accident. After a day of rest at home, he decided to go for a run. But from his first step, his left hip began hurting badly. Instead of stopping, Tafuto did what any committed endurance athlete would do: He tried to figure out how to run so it didn't hurt. He spent three hours trying to figure out how he could run without pain. Finally, he figured it out. He quickly developed a new gait so he could run without pain. And then he went for a run! During a return visit to the doctor a few days later, an x-ray revealed that he had fractured his hip. The doctor wanted to put him in a cast for three months, but Tafuto refused the cast and continued to work out (running with his new gait) until his hip healed. This is what we mean by dynamic leapfrogging: having a major problem and simply jumping over it. Putting the goal ahead of the problem.

Christopher Bear, Director of Sales Training, is a dynamic leapfrogger too. He was leading a cultural change at his company, Prudential. He was in charge of an effort to transform the sales approach. Change at senior levels propelled senior leaders to declare "mission accomplished" before the culture really was changed. Bear did not shrug his shoulders and say, "Oh well, another failed change initiative." He could have—it would not have affected his job and no one really would have cared. But he cared. And he knew the company would suffer if he didn't do something.

So he took it upon himself to lead a personal crusade. And we don't use the term loosely. He singlehandedly pushed forward the culture change. He worked day and night with a colleague to call, cajole, coach, inspire, and share stories with people so they would use the new sales tools that would change the culture and improve sales results. The bottom line is: It worked. Another year later his results showed continued success month-to-month and ROI above 600 percent. Bear's story is a strong lesson, reminding us to never doubt that one committed person, regardless of role and level, can bring about significant change in an organization.

John Morgan puts it this way: "I've always looked for people who are willing to go into a business situation and have the confidence to solve problems once they're 'on the ground.' I consider them 'smokejumpers.' They have the courage to jump into a tough situation without hesitation. But they also need to have self-confidence, self-awareness, and the ability to step back, breathe, and figure out how to make order out of chaos. The key to their success is learning by doing."

Plain hard work, elbow grease, stubbornness—whatever you want to call it, high-performance leaders don't underestimate it. They anticipate obstacles and instead of faltering or searching for a detour around them, they accelerate and clear the obstacles in one determined leap.

Change Calluses

Lawrence was once working out in the gym of a hotel in Washington, D.C. before a leadership training session, when he spotted a man running on the treadmill. Lawrence tried to match the runner's fast pace, but it was impossible to sustain it. After about 10 minutes, he looked down at the runner's feet. He couldn't believe it. The man was running in socks with no sneakers!

So Lawrence approached him and asked him how he managed it. First the runner looked surprised and looked down, and then said, "Oh yeah. I forgot." What he said next explained the unlikely comment: "I am from Kenya, here for a conference. I forgot my sneakers, but wanted to go running. In Kenya we run everywhere with no shoes—to school, to errands. Everywhere. It is just what we do."

The bottom line is that pushing through uncomfortable situations and extreme challenges is something that is learned through experience. You have to build up your calluses. Paul Beauchamp, partner at Deloitte & Touche, LLP says: "I believe the way you deal with change now is dependent of how much change you have gone through in the past. Experiencing change prepares you for the inevitable change in the future. In my business we might experience change over the life of our career by serving multiple accounts or multiple industries in multiple geographies. Professionals are always experiencing change as a result of the pace of promotion with the resulting responsibilities. Openness to that challenge is part of our fabric and through our ability to customize our own careers we are able to experience more or less change based on our specific goals. The amount of change you go through and the amount of client situations you'll see are limitless. It is common to never do the exact same thing for more than one year, which is unique to a professional services firm and may be hard to replicate in a corporate environment. A challenge in a corporate environment is to choose people who want to have a career experience that benefits from change, but also reward people whom the corporation needs to do repetitive tasks (many companies need them badly!)."

Curiosity

Franz Aatz says, "Rapid retooling means living in a permanent situation of insecurity and doubt. Many people feel overwhelmed by constant change at work. It is good to know that you are not alone! This knowledge helps to overcome stress and may promote willingness to go into uncharted territory. You have to cultivate a sense of curiosity about the work you do—or the work you want to do. Though satisfying your curiosity may not lead directly to results, it will help you make better decisions and come up with breakthrough ideas in the long term."

Worksheet: Building Your Personal Capacity for Rapid Retooling

What is your plan to sustain your energy?

- ☐ Work less?
- ☐ Play more?
- ☐ Get a job that fits your interests and values?
- ☐ Hire people who match your organization's requirements and culture?
- ☐ Make time to work on things you enjoy, but may not be in your job description?
- ☐ Learn stress management techniques, such as disconnecting to recharge?
- ☐ Ask for help?
- ☐ Implement the 80/20 rule?
- ☐ Telework?
- ☐ Other ideas____

What qualities do you need to hone in order to thrive in rapidly changing environments?

- ☐ Dynamic Leapfrogging
- ☐ Change Calluses
- ☐ Curiosity
- ☐ Other qualities that will help you succeed:__________________________

Chapter 7

Rapid Retooling in a High-Tech, Multicultural World

This chapter is focused on training initiatives that leading companies have used to lead or support rapid retooling. Because of the reduced cost of technology, some companies have their pick of virtual training programs that support quick development and global deployment of information and learning. We have also found many organizations are using very short, focused training sessions to minimize time away from employees' regular jobs. Finally, as organizations today are more educated about the importance of developing employees' business acumen, many are focusing on training that sharpens this kind of awareness and savvy. As such, we have broken up the stories and examples into these three sections:

- media training
- bricks-and-mortar training
- business-focused training.

Media Training

For Cisco, as a company that sells leading technology to connect people globally, it only makes sense to use that technology internally to gain competitive advantage. Cisco's rapid retooling challenge involved Millennials. First designed in 2001, its Cisco Sales Associates Program had to be revamped. The program's goal is to hire and train high-performing sales associates. The majority of associates in this program are 22 to 25 years old. It was costing way too much to get new sales associates up to speed because they had to be relocated to one of three training hubs, and Cisco had to pay for their travel and living expenses for 12 months.

Kate Day, director of the program, says, "We needed to rapidly retool not only our systems and processes, but also our people. We were fundamentally shifting a program from instructor-led training in three locations for 12 months, to something that had never been done on this scale before: virtual training for 20 global sites, in nine time zones, for 23 hours a day, running 12 tracks continuously. We had to address technology issues, our teams' skills, and the content of the program all at once. We had about 30 people supporting the program spread primarily between North America and Europe. They hadn't had a leader for six to eight months before I arrived. Oh, and we had to do it in four months!"

As it was, the sales associate program was siloed. The program wasn't just training—it included sourcing, onboarding, and developing and managing the performance of sales associates. Day's team included people representing each of these four functions. She had to break down silos within her team. She did this by focusing on business acumen and creating a team vision. "Business acumen was important. Everyone had to understand that everyone owned the budget for this program. They also started realizing that their actions had an impact on the entire program, not just their own function. The unifying goal was to hire sales associates, successfully guide them through training, and graduate them in 12 months ready to add revenue to Cisco.

"So by breaking down the silos, we got people energized and kept them energized because they're always trying new things. They don't get stale. The unifying goal also enables an environment of innovation because everyone is focused on the big picture: ensuring that the associate has an effectual experience and can graduate by passing the very strict graduation criteria at the end of 12 months."

When Day started her job, she hadn't had the opportunity to physically meet half the group. Because of the budget crunch she couldn't afford it. Even after 24 months in her new position, she hadn't met everyone physically, nor had she had her whole group in one place. How would she be able to establish an environment of trust and effectiveness?

Cisco's Telepresence technology certainly helps dramatically in making connections with people. "I never say 'Nice to meet you,' I say 'Nice to see you,' because after using the system it is hard to remember if I actually met them in person. It's really unsettling sometimes. It's just one of those things that I realize we're going to have to adapt to in the future."

Day also uses an internal personality system to connect with her team members. She or any leader can access data on anyone in the company that gives them insight into how that person thinks, what her natural talents are, and what drives her. “This really helped me understand and communicate and collaborate with my team a lot faster. I don’t think I could’ve accomplished what the group had to do in four months without this kind of help.”

Lisa Marie Fedele, who worked alongside Day on this project in a communications role, says the virtuality of her projects has forced her to be a better communicator. “I’ve not met any of the other people with whom I work. I always try to find information about someone I’m working with on our internal system because it helps me quickly understand how I need to communicate with that person and what he or she needs from our conversation. Because if you don’t do this, you get stuck in an endless loop of communicating: with the time zones being so different it’s really imperative that people leave a conversation with very clear objectives and know exactly what they need to deliver.”

The resulting program met the needs of the sales associates and Cisco. It combines self-directed learning, virtually facilitated learning sessions, on-site sessions with veteran sales associates, and assessments. They rolled out their new program in time, created a 24 percent cost reduction, and decreased the time before sales associates can be expected to create revenue for Cisco. Many graduates of this program are already outpacing other Cisco salespeople. And the bonus is that the graduates rave about the program.

Communicating ongoing marketing and operational changes to 4,000 employees is an ongoing challenge at Smokey Bones restaurants. Jay Bunkowske, Director of Training at Smokey Bones, uses the latest approaches to reach workers quickly. He creates YouTube videos on new menu items that a chef can watch on his or her mobile device right in the restaurant kitchen. Bunkowske also creates podcasts so employees can listen to information updates on their Apple devices. They also use ShiftNote, a web-based communication tool, to create and distribute documents that restaurants can print for educating and motivating employees. "The bottom line is you have to give them information to access when it is convenient for them, using technology."

Jiffy Lube, a subsidiary of Shell Oil, won the ASTD BEST Award in 2011 and 2012 for its top-notch training programs. It recently undertook a rapid retooling challenge that involved training 20,000 franchisee employees on procedures for collecting donations for the American Heart Association within two months. Ken Barber, the leader of the training department, explained, "Most of our training covers technician and store manager positions, and procedures for additional preventive maintenance services. In developing training for the American Heart Association, we were able to build on what we did well already: web-based courses. We developed a process called a 'Jiffy Lesson,' which was our internal language for a quick turnaround on a web-based course.

"In less than two months using this method, a storyboard was developed, video and graphics compiled, a script complete, voiceover recorded, a detailed review completed, and final web-based training (WBT) deployed. The course was then placed in the Jiffy Lube University LMS, which all employees can access. The deployment was supported with phone and email communications and the training was tracked to ensure its transfer to the job. The process has been repeated for similar program launches since its inspection."

Beyond technology, the key to their success, according to Barber, was silo-busting. "One thing that worked to our advantage was that the marketing department threw themselves into the project. They had tried to launch a similar effort on their own and it didn't work. So they came to us for help. The collaboration made a huge difference to the project's success. Since then, we consider marketing a strategic partner. They are more supportive of us when we need them because we helped them with a key objective."

The Jiffy Lesson process has been used for a number of marketing and business initiatives to great success. "Through this effort and the good work of Jiffy Lube store employees, $3 million was raised across North America during a three-year period. This year we are in the process of launching a similar campaign with the Muscular Dystrophy Association, with a goal to raise $1 million during a one-month window in the summer." At the time of publication, the MDA campaign was a big success, exceeding the goal by 15 percent!

Bricks-and-Mortar Training

Sometimes an intensely concentrated focus is the answer to urgent training needs. For example, imagine a leading retail chain closing its doors to customers for three hours of employee training. Seems unimaginable. But in 2008, Starbucks did just this to rapidly retool its entire U.S. workforce of 135,000 employees at 7,100 locations. The solution was low-tech but high-impact. When we talk in chapter 2 about the importance of focusing on a few priorities, this is what we mean. Feeling the squeeze from McDonald's and Dunkin' Donuts, as well the trend toward personal automatic espresso machines, Starbucks needed to refocus and reenergize its business in an area where it was losing ground: espresso. This all-hands-on-deck approach clearly demonstrates the company priorities to employees, and to customers for that matter.

"We will come together in an unprecedented event in our company's storied history," wrote Starbucks CEO Howard Schultz in a memo to employees. "We will close all of our U.S. company-operated stores to...share our love of coffee and the art of espresso. And in doing so, we will ...elevate the Starbucks experience for our customers. We are passionate about our coffee. And we will revisit our standards of quality that are the foundation for the trust that our customers have in our coffee and in all of us."

Starbucks continues to keep its eye on refocusing, reenergizing, and retooling its store managers. In his book *Onward*, Schultz says that employees are "the true ambassadors of our brand, the real merchants of romance and theater, and as such the primary catalysts for delighting customers." In this spirit, he began the Global Leadership Conferences for store managers in 2008. In October 2012, close to 10,000 store managers came together to learn about new technology, new products, and the brand they represent. The conference included a 400,000 square foot "Leadership Lab" experience. Managers walk through a multimedia experience, including thousands of live trees and pictures of native farmers, to see what goes into a cup of Starbucks coffee. Said Schultz at the Houston, Texas conference: "These next few days will give leaders the opportunity to reconnect with the heart of the company through community engagement, refining our coffee expertise, and perfecting the art of exceeding customer expectations."

Bricks-and-Mortar Training Rules

In the process of planning to optimize plant throughput, a Fortune 200 multinational manufacturing company realized that its supervisors needed training. Being a manufacturing company, they knew they had to make it short and practical, and settled on 20-minute rapid training sessions. Supervisors were taken off the floor for targeted practical sessions. Topics included employee motivation, stress reduction, labor laws, how to read reports, teamwork, and collaboration.

How did they manage to teach anything in 20 minutes? They came up with their own rules for these rapid training sessions:

- Rule 1: No PowerPoint allowed. Only flipcharts.
- Rule 2: Prepare two or three essential teaching points beforehand and questions to discuss; write on flipcharts.
- Rule 3: Give out handouts at the end of sessions.
- Rule 4: Leave them wanting more. If they do, we will prepare another session on this topic.

We have worked with an industrial global conglomerate to develop training that would support its effort to break down silos. It involves regularly bringing in its busy leaders from around the globe for face-to-face training. They are not only coming together to learn, but also to network, build relationships, and ultimately break down silos across their 7,000 employees. To reduce time and travel costs, we have created for them what we call a three-in-two program (three days of content delivered in two). It is a boot-camp type training program: 48 hours long, during which the group works continuously, except during short rests. The session focus is intense, and the leaders are not allowed any distractions.

All the feedback is positive. The leaders say they love the focus and intensity, appreciate the chance to meet people in other countries and share best practices, and even wish the session was longer! This is to the delight of our client. He would rather work them harder for a shorter period than work them less during a longer period. The program met the rapid retooling needs of silo busting and reenergizing their employees—all within 48 hours.

This was a learning experience for us as consultants. The traditional allowance for face-to-face training is nine-to-five in the classroom. Or perhaps self-directed e-learning. But in this case we saw that, with the right focus, motivation, and an engaging, hands-on program design, you can push participants hard and they will deliver the results you want. Another organization, a leading global financial services firm, also had a need for rapid training. They needed to train all their managers on creating an inclusive workforce. In two hours. They had to do this quickly for two reasons: First, there was some legal action brought against them. Second, taking highly-paid financial executives off their task of making money...well, it costs a lot of money. So how did they do it?

- Rule 1: Make it highly interactive to make it high impact.
- Rule 2: Get a leading expert to teach it.
- Rule 3: No lecture. Only challenging questions to discuss, some key content to teach, and a real-life case study to analyze.

These three rules enabled them to engage highly-educated, results-driven executives who were short on time and attention to give to the training. The program was so successful that the company rolled it out globally. And then, based on interest, they created a two-hour follow-up session.

RR Recommendation

Here are some ways to streamline your training and deliver it more quickly:

- Involve future participants to determine their most critical learning needs. The goal is to thoroughly align the content with the business problems.
- Develop content that is driven by interactive activities and discussions.
- Require pre-work for participants, which could include asking their manager how he or she thinks the content relates to current business problems.

Business-Focused Training

Two of the biggest challenges of all training departments is making the training relevant to the business and increasing the application of learning back on the job.

Google tackles these challenges by driving learning through bottom-up employee reviews of managers. The results of this review are then used to shape programs that help the managers improve. Customizing manager training in this way has a ripple effect, as managers are then better equipped to identify and address the needs of their employees.

To help employees understand the business of their business, Beam Global created the Beam Business Academy, in which employees learn about commercial activity in their industry. Sue Gannon, VP of Talent, Culture, and OD, explains how they make it more than a class. "At the end of training, people are set up in cross-functional teams to work on real commercial challenges. Leaders identify the key strategic challenges and have the teams work on them using the tools and theories from the training. They pursue solutions that will positively impact the company, with a deadline for presenting it to business leaders. This approach not only makes the training relevant to the business—it makes it critical to the business." As one of their executives says, "In essence the program helps employees focus on the question of 'How can I turn a dollar from every decision I make?'"

Michael, Learning Head for Sales and Underwriting at a leading insurance company, also focuses on empowering employees in their daily responsibilities. Instead of focusing on rolling out corporate-dictated training programs, "For any business area we work with, at the beginning of the year we discuss their business priorities, what it will take to achieve them, their assessment of their own ability, and how can we help them close any performance gaps," says Michael. This approach enables Michael and his team to create the type of change that the business needs to succeed.

Worksheet: Matching Training to Business Needs

Business Objective	Training Offering
1.	1.
2.	2.
3.	3.

At BMW Manufacturing, the question that drives training programs is, "To what extent do people on the line actually see their impact on the customer?" After all, when you are focused on putting in screws, you never see the end result. Werner Eikenbusch, Manager of Apprenticeship and Associate Training at the U.S. factory, said "We have run programs that connected people on the manufacturing line directly with customers. We would pull workers out into a half-day training session. It was taught by internal manufacturing managers to show that management is really serious about this. One thing we did, for example, is share customer letters that we received on the sales and marketing side. Another fun thing we did was to have them audit cars from the line. You can imagine that there are a lot of quality-control functions in a plant like this. So we had line workers audit a car that was prepared with minor quality defects. They had a checklist where they took note of flaws. Then we compared those with the official audit report. We showed them things that the auditor found that they didn't. They would say 'Wow, I didn't even know they looked at this.' It has had an amazing impact on motivation and increased attention to quality."

At FedEx, Bob Bennett, CLO, told us their training is very business-focused. "Part of what we're doing in trying to increase learning transfer is to integrate human resources services into the L&D organization. The HR advisors and reps out there, who normally are responsible for enforcing policies and procedures, took on coaching roles for our managers. They're no longer being measured on how many EEOs they have, or how many employee complaints. Because really, our goal is zero of those. So they actually spend time coaching our managers, reinforcing the leadership learning programs, and so forth. They still have traditional HR duties, but the amount of time they have to spend on them now is a lot less.

"We're also developing more tailored training solutions, and more individualized support. We're recognizing that a generic response to learning needs doesn't necessarily work for everybody. So we provide a lot of flexibility in our programs, and then provide a lot of individual attention.

"We have a 98 to 99 percent take rate (for our employee satisfaction survey), and it's all voluntary. We conduct the survey every two years. I can tell you, despite the recession, despite the economy, despite some of the things that FedEx has to do to cut costs, our survey score this year reached record heights. We continue to improve because we focus on the things that are important. For example, we changed the way we did our vehicle training, and we found that the number of accidents was reduced by a significant amount and millions of dollars gained in return savings, after the added costs of the program. We measure these programs specifically. We also measure courses that impact frontline managers. Do we do it for every program? No. But we always measure the ones that we believe have the greatest impact on the business operation."

Puma, the sports goods manufacturer, is dramatically redesigning itself, after years of sluggish business. Over the last few years it has become a leading "sport lifestyle" company. But the fast pace of global growth is driving Puma's systems and processes to their limits and with them its leadership and management resources.

Enter Roman Klein, hired as head of management development to try to establish a more cohesive development environment. Klein rolled out a new international leadership program aimed at improving management's focus on business priorities. One of the innovations was a new, very practical tool to deal with new leadership challenges: a peer-coaching process that they recently introduced across the organization. They teach the managers the process during the leadership program. The managers then form peer groups where they can get advice from their peers and collaboratively devise solutions. The peer groups are cross-functional to bring a fresher perspective to the discussions.

Managers now have a standardized process of asking for help. The process they teach in their training is:

1. Collect peer-coaching cases. Each person in the group gets his or her case listed on a flipchart. (10 minutes)
2. Participants choose the case they wish to discuss. (5 minutes)
3. Select facilitator, client, and peers. (2 minutes)
4. Client describes case and finishes with a question: "How can I....?" (10 minutes)
5. Peers ask questions to understand case.
6. Peers express assumptions. Facilitator records assumptions on flipchart. (10 minutes)
7. Client marks assumptions on flipchart with two colors: green=true; red=false. (2 minutes)
8. Peers develop solutions from assumptions; facilitator records solutions on flipchart. (10 minutes)
9. Client marks solutions on flipchart with two colors: green=realistic; red=unrealistic. (2 minutes)
10. Reflect on the process. What did the client and peers learn that they can take back to their daily work? (4 minutes)

Puma's peer coaching is particularly well-suited to accommodate the needs of a rapid retooling environment. Each leader or manager has instant access to help as he or she needs it. The peer-coaching process also removes the stigma of asking for help: Instead of being considered an admission of weakness, it is considered a critical element of Puma's collaborative, silo-busting culture; much more like an "in" lifestyle element. The tool also creates an environment of deeper trust, cooperation across departments, and a broader understanding of the business.

Puma also supports its continuous transformation through targeted communication. One example is its popular e-newsletter, "CATch up." Informative, interactive, and visually pleasing, it is an efficient tool to reach the Puma employee audience around the globe.

Making Training Fun and Exiting

As mentioned in the previous chapter, McDonald's trained 70,000 volunteers in a short timeframe for the 2012 Olympics. The London Organizing Committee of Olympic Games (LOCOG) was relying on them to help hire and train these volunteers to deliver expert customer service to millions of people over the course of the Olympics.

To do that, McDonald's helped conduct the largest non-military hiring process in the history of the U.K. And supported what may be the largest training sessions in U.K. history. The training was like a rock concert! Jez Langhorn, McDonald's VP of People, says, "We had one of our managers on stage in front of 10,000 people at a time at London Wimberley Stadium, talking about customer service and the importance of the role the Games Makers were going to play. Eleven thousand of those 70,000 volunteers were selected to be team leaders. So they would be tasked with looking after a number of volunteers. Those team leaders received some additional management and leadership training at our corporate university in London."

What was the secret of their success? Langhorn explained, "We leveraged our strength in training, and our training standards, methods, and procedures. You know, we've been training large numbers of people for years and years. So we built on that for the Olympics."

One key to rapidly retooling is leveraging your strengths. When faced with a big challenge, use what you are good at.

Final Thought: Why Isn't Work as Fun as This Class?

We recently led a very interactive executive workshop, and at the end, a participant asked a great question that led to an interesting discussion: "Why can't work be this fun?" The workshop was a "laboratory situation" simulating the executives' real work environment. At the time, they were facing many rapid retooling challenges at their company, which required them to:

- quickly accomplish an increasing number of tasks
- think outside the box
- make good decisions quickly
- address and overcome conflicts
- and of course, maximize profits.

During the simulation, the executives had a lot of fun! So, why did the fun stop the moment they returned to their desks?

Who better to ask than the executives themselves? Here is what they said:

1. Unlike in this class, roles and responsibilities are not clearly defined and assigned. This leads to power struggles, which can be detrimental to the success of a project and teamwork. Does everyone know who will be doing what to achieve the goals? Where are there overlaps? Where do people need to help each other? Where do people need to stay out of each other's way?

2. Unlike in this class, we are afraid of making mistakes. There may be high stakes in the real-life scenario, while a simulation is, of course, free of pressure. High stakes generates fear, which cripples productivity and innovation. If we are not willing to take some risks, we are not being creative, and we are definitely not having fun.

3. Unlike in this class, we have impossible time constraints. We may already be so overwhelmed that no matter how fun a new project may be, the reality of our workloads doesn't let us pour our passion into it. We already know that we'll be forced to deliver subpar work, which is just the opposite of having fun!

4. Unlike in this class, there is a lack of full involvement. Often we are approached for help when a project is already half done or when it has run into problems. This partial involvement will never generate high levels of ownership and enthusiasm.

5. Unlike in this class, there are corporate politics at play. We can't always speak our minds. We don't dare to express some opinions or ideas. We don't dare to address conflicts. No fun!

6. Unlike in this class, our virtual world makes collaboration difficult. There are a lot of emotional landmines embedded in virtual collaborations. We can't always interpret other people's reactions, strong bonds are difficult to form, and we may feel less urgency to apply our full focus and energy to the project.

7. Unlike in this class, there are often no clear team objectives. There is a lack of team focus (or even worse, the focus is on individual success at the expense of the team). This kind of competition and lack of collective focus makes effective teamwork impossible.

8. Unlike in this class, the rewards and recognition are not motivating. Is there a system in place for recognizing individual and team accomplishments? Do employees find the rewards attractive? Are the behaviors and achievements that are rewarded in line with the team's goals?

9. Unlike in this class, there is a lack of trust. Employees should place trust in their peers and in their leadership.

So the final question we have for our readers is, "What can you do to promote fun in the real workplace?" Despite the endless unpredictable challenges of today's business environment, if you can implement the advice in this book (see the numbered list for cliff notes!), you can create a fun, energizing, and productive workplace, which continually and organically retools itself.

References

The Asking Formula. http://www.theaskingformula.com/

eePulse. http://www.eepulse.com/

Gray, P., "As Children's Freedom Has Declined, So Has Their Creativity," *Psychology Today*, September 17, 2012, http://www.psychologytoday.com/blog/freedom-learn/201209/children-s-freedom-has-declined-so-has-their-creativity.

Jennings, J. (2012). *The Reinventors: How Extraordinary Companies Pursue Radical Continuous Change.* New York: Penguin Group.

Johansen, B. (2009). *Leaders Make the Future: Ten New Leadership Skills for an Uncertain World.* San Francisco, CA: Berrett-Koehler.

Mark Owen, interview by Scott Pelley, *60 Minutes*, CBS, February 24, 2013.

PeopleNRG. (2011). *Leading Global Change Best Practice Report.* Princeton, NJ: PeopleNRG.

PeopleNRG. (2012). *Leading Global Change Best Practice Report.* Princeton, NJ: PeopleNRG.

PeopleNRG. (2013). *The 19 Steps to Lead Employees Over the River of Fear.* Princeton, NJ: PeopleNRG.

Polsky, L. Keep the Change, *HumanResourcesIQ,* HumanResourcesiq.com.

Torrance Tests of Creative Thinking (TTCT). http://ststesting.com/2005giftttct.html

About the Authors

Since 2008, **Antoine Gerschel** and **Lawrence Polsky** have educated and inspired over 60,000 leaders on five continents through their speeches, coaching, training, and books. Some of the companies they have recently assisted with implementing rapid change include AES Corporation, Convergex, Canberra, Con Edison, the City of New York, Dell, LG Electronics, Guard Insurance, Maxim Healthcare Services, Merrimack Pharmaceuticals, NASA, the U.S. Patent and Trademark Office, UBS, the United States Army, and WalMart. Their previous bestselling books include *Perfect Phrases for Communicating Change, Say YES! to Change: 27 Strategies to Motivate Yourself and Your Team*, and *Perfect Phrases for Conflict Resolution*. Lawrence also writes a column, "Keep the Change!" on humanresourcesiq.com. They are managing partners at PeopleNRG, a Princeton-based consulting firm that maximizes the performance of teams facing rapid change. To access additional rapid retooling tools such as instructional videos, webinars, and articles, you can follow them on Twitter @peoplenrg or visit them at www.rapidretooling.com or www.peoplenrg.com.